FIVE WOMEN

Five Women

TONY PARKER

faber and faber

This edition first published in 2013
by Faber and Faber Ltd
Bloomsbury House, 74–77 Great Russell Street
London WC1B 3DA

Printed by Books on Demand GmbH, Norderstedt

All rights reserved
© Tony Parker, 1965

The right of Tony Parker to be identified
as author of this work has been asserted in accordance
with Section 77 of the Copyright, Designs and Patents Act 1988

This book is sold subject to the condition that it shall not, by way of
trade or otherwise, be lent, resold, hired out or otherwise circulated
without the publisher's prior consent in any form of binding or cover other than
that in which it is published and without a similar condition including this
condition being imposed on the subsequent purchaser

A CIP record for this book is available from the British Library

ISBN 978–0–571–30426–4

For my sisters

KAY & PAULINE
with love

The proper examination of recidivist cases is only in its infancy . . . Such systematic work as has been done on unselected groups indicates that a very considerable number of them suffer either from pathological stigmata or have acquired these stigmata through penological mishandling. Until proper measures of investigation have been applied it is really absurd to draw hard and fast conclusions on the subject.

EDWARD GLOVER

The Concept of Recidivism

(*By kind permission of Edward Glover and the Imago Press Publishing Co.*)

While the precise aetiology of delinquency and crime must vary with each individual case, the broad conditions which generate and stimulate them are well known. It is the final eradication of such conditions which can alone provide the only sure guarantee against the continued presence of anti-social behaviour which involves the community in expense which is not limited to the financial sphere.

TERENCE MORRIS

The Criminal Area

(*By kind permission of Terence Morris and Messrs Routledge & Kegan Paul*)

CONTENTS

	A NOTE ON THE AUTHOR	1
	INTRODUCTION	5
I	Carol Dean, age 19, *Robbery*	15
II	Diane Richards, age 24, *Forgery*	49
III	Joe Bishop, age 30, *Burglary*	81
IV	Miss McDonald, age 40, *Fraud*	105
V	Janie Preston, age 60, *Larceny*	137
Appendix	Millie, age 17	166
	BIBLIOGRAPHY	187

A Note on the Author

TONY PARKER
1923–1996

'Oral history' is what we call works made by a writer who conducts extensive in-depth interviews with a subject or subjects; then edits, structures and refines the verbatim transcripts so as to produce a seamless account of the subject(s) in their own words. Oral historians absent themselves from the texts they make, though their personal interests and skills will tend to shine through. At its best, oral history possesses unique qualities of immediacy and narrativity; and there has been no more admired practitioner of the form in English than Tony Parker.

Parker's reputation is founded upon eighteen discrete works of oral history which he published across a professional writing career that began in 1962 and ended with his death in 1996 (though one further work, a study of his great American counterpart Studs Terkel, appeared posthumously). Obituaries for Parker served a powerful reminder of the high esteem in which he was held by colleagues and contemporaries, both for his qualities as a man and for his incredible dexterity as an interviewer and editor. Colin Ward wrote in the *Independent*, 'His triumphs were the result of his gentleness and modesty, which led the most taciturn or suspicious of people to open up with confidences they would not dream of revealing to more self-assertive questioners.' 'The power of his silence', Roger Graef noted in the *Guardian*, 'created a vacuum which invited others to fill it.' More than one elegist cited the famous words of Parker's close friend the psychologist Anthony Storr: 'Tony Parker's ears are a national treasure.'

Parker excelled as a silent witness, a man who listened with care; but he was also a man of strong personal and political conviction, rooted in the left. Oral history has no inherent caste or complexion but it is probably fair to say that Parker was especially moved by examples of injustice, inequality and unfairness in our society, and was driven to give a voice to people otherwise neglected or marginalised. His work doesn't sit in any traditional academic canon of sociology, ethnography or criminology. But for anyone who read Parker's matchlessly intimate portraits of these marginal figures – from convicted murderers to homeless people and unmarried mothers – the effect was to transform our perceptions of the human society and systems that we share.

Tony Parker was born in Stockport on 25 June 1923, the son of a bookseller. His mother died when he was four. He began to write poems and plays in his late teens. Called up to military service early in the Second World War he declared himself a conscientious objector and, in lieu, was sent to work at a coal-mine in the North East, where he observed conditions and met people who influenced him hugely. After the war he began to work as a publisher's representative and, voluntarily, as a prison visitor – the latter another important stimulus to his subsequent writings. It is believed that Parker was especially galvanised, too, by the infamous case of Christopher Craig and Derek Bentley, in which nineteen-year-old Bentley (illiterate, epileptic and judged by his national service examiner to be 'mentally substandard') was hanged for the murder of a police officer, though the fatal shot had been fired by sixteen-year-old Craig.

After Parker happened to make the acquaintance of BBC radio producer Paul Stephenson, and imparted his growing interest in the lives, opinions and self-perceptions of the prisoners he had met, he was given by Stephenson the opportunity to record an interview with a particular convict for broadcast on the BBC. The text of the interview was printed in the *Listener*, and spotted by the publishers Hutchinson as promising material for a book. This duly emerged as *The Courage of His Convictions* (1962), for which Parker and the career criminal 'Robert Allerton' (a pseudonym) were jointly credited as authors. In the coherence of the book's organisation; in the candour and insight elicited from the subject; in the very human quality of pawky humour; and in the discernible intent to challenge prejudices and illuminate neglected or hidden aspects of our society – the book exhibits all of the virtues that were to make Tony Parker's body of work so vital and cherishable.

So much of Parker's oeuvre has been out of print for so long that Faber Finds is hugely pleased and proud to be returning a dozen of his titles to availability in 2013. These are *The Courage Of His Convictions* (1962), *The Unknown Citizen* (1963), *The Plough Boy* (1965), *Five Women* (1965), *A Man Of Good Abilities* (1967), *People of the Streets* (1968), *The Twisting Lane: Some Sex Offenders* (1969), *The Frying Pan: A Prison and its Prisoners* (1970), *In No Man's Land: Some Unmarried Mothers* (1972), *The People of Providence: A Housing Estate and Some of Its Inhabitants* (1983), *Soldier, Soldier* (1985) and *Red Hill: A Mining Community* (1986). As such, Parker's vital invitation to all of us to think, and think again, has been renewed: readers old and new are warmly commended to take up the challenge.

Richard T Kelly
Editor, Faber Finds
March 2013

INTRODUCTION

On a cold spring morning in 1963 five women came out of Holloway Prison. They all had long records: between them they had been convicted seventy-three times, and had spent a total of nearly a hundred years in prison. An administrative change brought them unexpected remission and immediate release from Preventive Detention, a sentence given to habitual criminals not so much for a particular offence as to protect society by keeping them in prison for a long time.

The subject of habitual offenders and long sentences was one I had become particularly interested in while writing *The Unknown Citizen**; and I was commissioned by the British Broadcasting Corporation to write a radio-programme about these five women preventive detainees. I hoped to interview them as soon as possible after their release, and talk to them about their hopes and intentions and fears; and then get in touch with them again after a few months had passed, and try to find out how their experience of reality had matched their expectation of it.

Although five were discharged from prison that morning, I was able to meet only four: the other immediately disappeared. No more was heard of her until several weeks later when she appeared in court charged with shoplifting, where to her surprise she was put on probation by a magnanimous judge. Yet even then I was still unable to meet and talk with her: within a fortnight she committed a further offence, and when

* Hutchinson, 1963

she came to court this time not unexpectedly she was sent back to prison.

I met the four women, individually and on different days, at the offices of the Women's Division of the Central After-Care Association in a quiet mews near Victoria Station. With each of them, as with every other prisoner released after a long sentence, the only subject at first was prison. After a time we were able to move on to a discussion of their past criminal activity; and finally we could begin to talk about themselves as individuals, and to make the recordings. I had about an hour and a half's conversation with each, and arranged to meet them again in about six months' time.

'The strongest immediate impression' I noted at the end of the week in which I had met them, 'was that they all seemed to be physically so small, although two of them were actually taller than I am. They seemed airless and crumpled, like only partially-inflated balloons; they filled-out very slowly as we talked. There was nothing about any of them that suggested a life of crime was ever anything but sad, dull and drab; nothing anywhere glamorous or romantic. Whatever men think of when they start to imagine "women"– sexual attraction, mystery, excitement, warmth, enchantment, pleasure—no longer lives at these addresses: they are hollow, pathetic, living as they do in deep separate wells of lonely bitterness. It is difficult to understand how anyone could ever have felt condemnatory towards them, or angry; difficult to feel anything at all for that matter now, or respond to them in any way. Perhaps it can only be done by looking long at each one and trying to imagine her as a person—as mother, daughter, sister, wife, mistress; by trying to imagine a relationship, and how one would feel if one were involved in any of those ways, tied by that sort of bond . . . How else get close and learn feeling for those who have forgotten how to feel?

'Of the four, two are almost ruins physically, and sending them out of prison seems as irrelevant to their need and condition as sending them in to it must have done in the first place. They are not being set free by being released; they are turned out and rejected and abandoned. Of the other two, one is clearly a menace and freeing her also bears no relation to her true condition. Release may be an unavoidable necessity; but it is dangerous to society. And for the fourth also prison must always have been irrelevant. She seems almost to have wanted punishment throughout her life and to have sought it: no one seems to know why, least of all herself. And every time she has had it, she has been driven further and further back into herself, out of sight, out of reach. Punishment and resentment deepen and worsen her condition.

'Meeting them at twenty-four hour intervals one after another, it was striking how alike they all seemed to be at the beginning of each interview. They have all been pressed so hard and so long in the depersonalising mould of imprisonment. It makes them all seem only slightly-varying copies of the same person. And perhaps, in a way, that is what they are.'

Beneath the notes I made a personal and completely subjective estimate, expressed as a percentage, of what I thought each one's chances were of staying out of prison until we met again.

* * * * *

When that time came, only one out of the five remained; two had died: and the other had gone back to prison after committing further offences, rejoining the one whom I had never even had the chance of meeting.

The one who was left was in fact she whose chances of surviving I had estimated lowest of all, at 20%. For someone with a record as long as hers to remain out of prison and refrain from criminal activity as she had done was certainly unusual; and her success was due to a combination of factors which included among many others effort, luck and perceptive after-care supervision.

After the second meeting, and the subsequent broadcast of the radio-programme, I continued to see her. Often when we talked together I began to wonder . . . how it was that someone should live the sort of life she had done: what she had been like when she was younger—in her forties, her thirties, her twenties and teens: what so much imprisonment, given so frequently, had done to her: why and for what reason women at different ages came to be in prison, and what effect it had on them: who they were and what they were like...

What she herself had been like at different ages, it was no longer really possible to tell. She had spent over a third of her adult life in prison, and in common with others who have spent that much time there and more, she had no people anywhere with whom she had been in continuous contact for any length of time. She had no relatives living, and no friends; during the whole of her last sentence she had had no visits from anyone, no letters, no Christmas or birthday cards. No one knew her, and her past could now only be fragmentarily and imperfectly recreated by her own memory, which was faulty and confused. The girl and the young woman who had grown into what she now was had gone and were lost sight of, and could never be recalled.

But other women exist, at different ages and different

stages of their criminal careers. I began to meet some of them. Not all will end their lives like she is now, almost completely separated from society, friendless and alone; nor did they have the same kind of beginning. But they are all, whatever their age, as she was—the sort of woman who is sent to prison. And we might ask ourselves one day perhaps whether it does them, or us, any good to continue to punish them in this way, regularly and consistently, at the rate of over two thousand a year. We should ask it not because they are women and should therefore be judged and treated differently; but simply because they are people. In women can be seen more clearly the marks of mishandling and suffering—the 'stigmata' referred to by Dr. Edward Glover. But they are inflicted also on men, in far greater number. We continue to imprison *people*, without real knowledge of what we are doing to them.

I met just over twenty women in all, over a period of two years, and this book is about a small number of them, chosen from different age-groups and at different points on the scale of experience of imprisonment. The first is only just beginning; she has been in prison once. But she knows its terrors now and is no longer afraid; what comes after can never be quite so bad. A few years older, the second has already been in prison three times; at twenty-four she seems condemned to a life of crime and can find no other way of living, though she struggles desperately. The third has now almost given-up. She has always been a reject, an outcast: what does it really matter what happens to her; and who cares? She asks, and hears no answer. The fourth appears almost inevitably destined to receive a very heavy sentence before long, because no one will be able to think what else can possibly be done with her if she gets into trouble again. And the fifth is the woman from thinking about whom the book began: she is old, she is hidden, she has taken all the punishment we can give. In experience of imprisonment she might almost be the sum of all the others; and they all, perhaps, in a way be part of her ...

There is, finally, a sixth person. She is a girl, not a woman; and she is not at any point in a criminal career. In fact she is not a criminal, and never has been. But she is included because she has been in prison; and it is not as widely known as it might be that girls do go to prison who have committed no crimes.

* * * * *

Without the help of the Central After-Care Association (which has since been assimilated into the newly-established Probation and After-Care Service) it would have been quite impossible to write this book. Miss Mary Stone, the Director of the Women's Division of C.A.C.A., has been a friend for several years and an adviser from whom I constantly learn; I owe her much more than I can ever express. Miss D. Love, one of the principal After-Care Supervisors in the Women's Division, has given me limitless help; my debt to her is very great, and I thank her with both affection and respect.

I must also thank the Prison Department of the Home Office for permission to visit Holloway Prison, and the Governor, Mrs. Kelley, and several members of her staff, for making the visit an informative one; Miss Mary Hamilton; Mr. Neville Vincent; Dr. Peter Scott; Mr. Gordon Cool; Mr. J. Roche of Imhof's; Mr. Paul Stephenson of the B.B.C.; Mr. Harold Harris and Mr. Graham Nicol of Hutchinson; the libraries of the Howard League and the Institute for the Study and Treatment of Delinquency; the Brentwood branch of the Essex County Library; Mrs. M. E. Gravett for typing the manuscript; and my wife Margery, as always, for her help and understanding.

And most of all my gratitude is due to the women who talked to me about themselves and their lives so freely and directly, who gave me so much of their time and answered so many questions. Not all of them appear now in this book: the names of those who do have been changed, and so have a few other identifiable details. But their words are set down as they said them, without additions or alterations; though most of my own questions of course have been omitted.

This, I hope, conveys what they wanted to say; and shows them, human, as they are.

TONY PARKER

Brentwood, Essex

*The happiest women
have no history*

GEORGE ELIOT

CAROL DEAN

ROBBERY

AGE: *19*
NUMBER OF CONVICTIONS: *2*
TOTAL TIME SPENT IN PRISON: *1 year 6 months*

1

Carol Dean

Parts of the East End of London are as they were twenty years ago, at the end of the Second World War. After the bombs had stopped falling they were tidied of rubble, and left.

The wide and barren bomb-sites remain infertile, with streets running across their emptiness, and nothing but kerb-stone and pavement on each side. Wrecks of buildings where people once lived stand open to the sky, fireplaces one above the other in the central interior walls showing how many floors they used to have. The inhabitants live now even more closely packed, between the spaces that enemy destruction made; in boroughs that have the highest population-densities and the lowest property-rateable values in London.

Off the main traffic arteries the crowded and cosmopolitan shopping streets have only a few new shops. Many of the old ones are abandoned and boarded-up, or being used for some purpose other than retailing. Over their impenetrable fascias signboards carry uniformative wording like 'All Kinds Of Supplies', 'Retail Warehousemen' and 'General Manufacturers To Trade', to indicate makers of cardboard cartons, tobacconists' wholesalers, and tiny tailoring workshops with staffs of four. 'Machinist Quickly Wanted' is scrawled on an envelope pinned to the jamb of a painted-over shop door, 'Can Be Earned At Once Up To 25 Pound A Week'.

Everywhere there are these signs and notices; temporary and permanent, they proliferate. Outside a used-clothing and footwear shop, adjacent and contradictory statements: 'Best Prices Given For Cast-Offs' and 'Buy Here: Nowhere Cheaper'. In a barber's doorway a neatly-painted board: 'Jack's Hygienic Saloon'. Hand-written in straggling white lettering across a baker's window: 'Bigels All Fresh Here Today'. Carefully lettered and measured-out on a white card in the window of a dress-material shop: 'Any Leangth Cut That Customer Requires'. Chalked on a blackboard outside a greengrocer's: 'Fresh Well-Matured Herring'.

Betting-shops, junk-furniture shops, herbalists, newsagents, ironmongers, electrical and household goods shops—those selling expensive things like record-players radios and tape-recorders that are easily movable have permanent thick wire grilles over their windows—most of them seem to be open all day and night, every day of the week. Between them and in some places in rows next to one another, are numberless cafés with steamed-up windows, plastic curtains, bamboo screens, cigarette advertisements, menus, coloured lights, dim lights, or no lights at all. Some cater for one particular national or racial section of the community—'Chan Man House, Oriental Delicacies', 'Veeri's Curried Specialities', 'Fred's: Egg and Chips': others try for heterogeneous custom, offering 'Dinner No. 1: Salt Beef, Noodles, Sweet, Tea. Dinner No. 2: Fish, Spaghetti, Sweet, Tea. Dinner No. 3: Chicken and Chips, Tea. All 4/6d. each'.

Many others hardly bother either to cook or to sell food: they provide only tea, coffee, Coca-Cola and perhaps sandwiches. The attraction is the juke-box: the place is a meeting point for young people, where they can spend little money and a lot of time, and no one bothers them. On the door pillar of one popular place, someone has painstakingly scratched in the stonework the unchangeable list of priorities: The Rolling Stones, The Blue Jeans, The Kinks, The Animals, The Honeycombs. And underneath, down at the bottom of the column after a space, as a calculated insult the list continues: The Mojos, The Beatles ...

The streets are crowded in the evenings till after midnight. People stand, talk, move: in and out of the pubs and cafés, congregating in changing groups of noise in pools of light outside shop windows; they chatter, laugh, shout. Sometimes friendly words and sometimes not. White, yellow, brown, black, Gentile, Jew. Africans in groups enjoy one another's jokes and whistle at passing girls. Anxious Lascars press bell-pushes outside little locked doors between shops, move away muttering to each other, and try ineffectually to peer through gaps in curtained windows, searching for familiar faces or agreeable girls. Grey-haired and shawled old Jewish ladies swamp each other with vehement words, then break off for silent disapprovals mutually agreed. Brass-studded-black-leather jacketed fair haired youths with their hands in their pockets and bunched shoulders slouch slowly along the pavement in groups, giving everyone plenty of time to move out of their way. Behind them trail girls in blue jeans, short coats and high-heeled boots, their long straight hair hanging in a curtain round their faces: they giggle and try to push each other into the boys.

There seems always a bare edge on the night, as if

those who jostle it will be in danger.

In the daytime the atmosphere is muted, sheathed; there are older and less confident people about, there are things to do connected with earning a living. A few people stand outside the betting-shops, a few at corners. Middle-aged women with four children are shopping, elderly men come out looking for a breath of air, an ounce of tobacco and a talk. Most conversation is about work. A wooden cart, painted bright green and pulled by a small white horse glides along on its balloon-tyres towards the market.

If you turn away from the main thoroughfares and walk down the side streets most of them seem soon to peter out after a short row of old two-storied houses into the vacant windblown spaces which mark where the bombs once fell.

Beyond, rehousing has begun. The modern blocks of flats eighteen or twenty storeys tall rise up singly or in clustering twos and threes from the flat ground like giant cacti in the Arizona desert. It will be years before schemes are complete, before the wartime scars have been covered; and still more years before the worse disfigurations of slum housing have been razed, reordered and rebuilt. Meantime thousands live in old buildings crowded between bomb-sites and austere concrete towers of new flats, in properties which should have been demolished decades ago; but which, existing still, inhabited and over-crowded, bring in rents of considerable size for the investment-companies which own them.

When they were erected in the early years of the century, they were called variously 'Mansions', 'Dwellings' or 'Buildings', and they offered living conditions which were considered quite good for the working classes. They were madequate then the passing of time has made them primitive. Knowing that it cannot be long before they are pulled down, landlords have given up any idea of maintaining them, and they are allowed to moulder: roofs leak, concrete facings corrode and fall, fire hazards are ignored, dirt accumulates.

They are large gloomy dirty-red brick groups of identical four-storey blocks, five or six arranged closely parallel, and bound into a whole of ugly uniformity by a perimeter wall. Within them are a hundred, two hundred, sometimes as mary as five hundred two-room flats. Between each block is a concrete yard, off which lead entrances to stone stairways which run up, four or five to a block, to each floor. The stairways are open to the weather front and back, each landing merely railed-off with a low ironwork fence. None of the flats has water. On each landing are three large stone sinks in a communal washroom to which water—cold only—is piped; next door to the washroom is a toilet. Both are used by up to a dozen families. Clothes that have been washed must be taken up to the roof and hung out to dry on the maze of wire washing-lines which criss-cross the cluttered grimy spaces between the rows of brick chimney stacks and the tangle of TV aerials.

The concrete yard below is a play area for children, and dogs; it is also a tip for old mattresses, empty packing-cases, broken milk-bottles and any old pieces of newspaper which have been blown in by the wind. On each side stretch up the high soiled walls of the buildings with their small windows, and their mosaic of outside plumbing which in winter unfailingly freezes-up, bursts, and drips or deluges with the thaw.

Each block—A, B, C, D, E, F—is individualised only by the white-painted capital letter on its end wall. Over the stairway entrances from the yards are the numbers of the flats the stairway leads to: 1—48, 49—96, 97—142, and so on. At night a dim light-bulb burns in some of the entrances, and on one or two of the landings. So an attempt can be undertaken to distinguish between one block and another, one floor and another, and to find one particular flat where someone lives . . .

'Come on Tuesday' she had said. 'You'll easy find it, it's the last floor of the third block. But if you get lost, just ask anyone about, they'll tell you where Number 741 is.'

It was late at night in winter, it was dark, and the cold rain was pitching down with determination. Probably what she had said had been the third floor of the last block; there wasn't anyone about to ask; knocked-at doors remained shut. Inside an entrance-way from one of the yards, a man and woman feverishly clutched at each other, oblivious; inside another, and stepped in, was a smelly pile of excreta, possibly canine.

It took time, the first time, to find Number 741.

Carol is 19, short, stocky, large-boned, with long black hair that falls about her shoulders and flops forward to surround and sometimes cover her face. Going out to somewhere special she wears it up, held with combs and with a spit-curl in front of each ear, so that she looks imperious, like a Flamenco dancer. But usually it is not given much attention; she looks wild and gypsy-like and often while she is talking she is almost hidden from view behind it, showing only the gleam of her deep-set dark blue eyes and her white teeth. Then suddenly remembering something that amuses her she will toss her head, her hair will fly back, and her face will emerge smiling, wide-mouthed and sallow.

She has a boy friend who lives with her when he is

around, and provides her with money. Sometimes she works herself in one of the small local tailoring shops. So there are occasions when she has money, and things are not difficult; but other times she has nothing, she is cold because she has no oil for the stove, and hungry because with what money she has she buys cigarettes rather than something to eat. But she is strong like a young animal, full of spirit, never worries. 'Me? No, I've no troubles, I don't let life get me down, what's the use? Enjoy it while you're young, you're only young once, aren't you? I get by.'

It seems to generate all her movements, this determination to accept and indulge and enjoy sensuously, and gives them an undercurrent of lustiness, of restrained ebullience. She smokes incessantly, inhaling deeply, gesticulates fiercely with hands and arms, as she struggles sometimes to put into words what she is trying to say. Her voice is low with a rasping sexiness, thick with smoke; her laugh crackling and constant. She talks about herself and her life honestly and directly, and without pretence.

If you ask how long she has lived in the East End she replies without thinking 'Oh always.' She has in fact been there for only just over four years, but is not speaking untruthfully or pretending. To her it genuinely feels now like 'always'. Until she arrived she was never an individual to herself, had no sense of personal identity or of belonging in any place.

Her family live in the West country; she was born there, and grew up speaking with that accent. But now it is impossible to tell she was not born and brought up Cockney: she uses the speech rhythm unthinkingly, the expressions and accent as easily and naturally as if they were and always have been her own. 'Straight up!' and 'My Life!' she ejaculates, but not too often nor at consciously thought-out moments; she speaks of 'my bruvver', of something being 'the trufe', of telling someone 'to turn it up'.

A true denizen of the East End, she has too the same confined-community sense as its own citizens have. All her life has been lived within an area less than a mile square, and she talks about Mile End, Shoreditch and Bethnal Green as though they were distant provincial towns. And herself, she doesn't go much on them, either . . .

Move? Nah, never, I can't seem to like them places, know what I mean? It's the people, I fink, they're different some'ow, not like us rarnd 'ere, know what I mean? Perhaps when I'm older, you know, when I'm a real old woman of thirty an' that, wiv lots of kids, then I might move art that way. But not before, I just can't see mesel' doin' it some'ow, nah. It's difficult to explain, but I feel I belong 'ere. I 'onestly don't want to go nowhere else, I don't want to live nowhere else or anyfink like that. All me friends are rarnd 'ere, me bruvver's 'ere, me sister, me boy friends . . . Nah, I just couldn't do it.

Maybe for them I might move, if I had kids; I might move for them to a nicer area, somewhere art in the country a bit, or down the seaside, Sarfend or somefin like that. But not until they was growed-up—an' I expect by then they'd have got to like it 'ere, so they wouldn't want to move no more theirselves, would they? Anyway, if I 'ad kids that'd mean I was married and settled down, wunnit, and if I did that, I'd be settled down wiv a boy from rarnd 'ere, wun I? So 'e wouldn't want to move, and I wouldn't, so I don't expect we'd move then, even, would we?

I dunno, this just seems like where I belong, like I've

always lived 'ere among all these people. They're my people, I belong wiv them, they're easy to get on wiv, natural, they don' look down on yer or want yer to be any different from what you are. As soon as I come 'ere I felt that, I did, the very first day, straight up.

Why did I come? Well me sister was 'ere you see, she'd married a Londoner and come to live 'ere, and I come to live wiv 'er. Let's have another cup of tea, shall we, and then I'll start at the beginnin', where I was born and that. Oh I must feed Steve's tropical fish for 'im first, he'll go potty if he comes back and finds I 'aven't been feeding them proper. 'Is fish is the main fing he finks abart. Right, that's it, well let's see if we can get started, all right?

I was born in 1946 in a little village in Cornwall. My dad's a coalman—you know, driving a lorry and delivering bags of coal. My mum had sixteen children. Three died. There are four older than me—two older sisters and two older brothers—and eight younger, so you could say I was about the middle. None of the family's ever been in trouble except me and one of my older brothers, Jimmy, who went away for 15 months once. My other brother's still down there at home, working as a coalman, same as me dad. We're a big family and well-known in the village, of course, because there's so many of us.

When you say you come from a village in Cornwall, everyone thinks of the seaside, don't they, they imagine you must have come from somewhere like off a picture-postcard. But I didn't: our village was right inland, in the middle of the country, in a place no one ever came to visit or look at. It was a dump, really, a few tumble-down houses round a worked-out tin-mine, all very untidy and dirty.

With so many children, there was never a lot of money to go round, and on top of that my dad is quite a big gambler, always having bets every day, so whenever she can my mum works too. She's got a job in the bakery in the village and works there regular, stopping off now and again to have another kid, then back again as soon as she can to work. She likes it, though, she likes working: she's a very jolly sort of person, and they think a lot about her at the bakery.

My father, he's nice too, he's very strict but he's nice, and he and mum are very very fond of each other and all the kids. I don't think anyone's a special favourite unless it's the newest one each time, the baby, know what I mean? My father always made us go to church regular every Sunday: if we didn't we was punished by not being allowed to go out for the rest of the week, or something like that. When I was little I was quite frightened of him because he was so strict, but as I've grown up of course I've lost that.

Me and my sisters used to do awful things to him sometimes. He had to set off very early in the mornings on his rounds, and before he went he used to write out his day's bets on a piece of paper, and leave it on the kitchen table with the money, for mum to take and put it on for him when she went to work. We used to sneak downstairs as soon as we heard him go out of the house, tear-off the bottom half of the paper and keep half the money and divide it up among ourselves. Of course some days one of his horses on the torn-off part of the list would win, and he'd come home at night asking mum if she'd collected for him; she'd say she knew nothing about it, he hadn't written the horse on the list, and there'd be a terrible row. We were in bed by then, and we could hear it going on downstairs, and we were killing ourselves laughing, we were really dreadful, we were.

None of us got a lot of schooling. The only school was a long way away, three or four miles over the moors, and with dad and mum both being out at work we often used to stay at home because neither of them was there to send us off. My eldest sister Irene was the one who stayed at home to look after all the kids, but she was only fifteen and she never used to bother if we said we didn't want to go to school. She hadn't liked it much herself, so she didn't try very hard to make the rest of us go.

Now and again the school's inspector would come round to see me dad—and he used to shout at him, and tell him to clear off and not come pushing his nose into other people's business. He's a big man, my dad, and the inspector was only small and I think he was frightened of him.

I didn't like school any more than Irene had done, in fact I hated it. I couldn't learn anything, not a thing, I hadn't got the brain for it, and I was always getting into trouble. After I was twelve, I stopped going altogether, and my dad said well if I wasn't learning I might as well be earning, so he got me a job at a big house in the next village. Dad said to tell the woman I was 14.

They were well-to-do people, I think she was some kind of nurse, or had been when she was younger. Anyway, she and her husband ran this big house as one of them places, what do you call them, convent homes—no, convalescent homes—for old rich people who aren't all that ill, but want to go somewhere and be looked after and made a fuss of and pay a lot of money for it.

The woman had three children herself; two of them were away at boarding school, but she had a little girl of three that I was employed to look after during the day. If it was fine I had to take her out for walks, or in her push chair; and if it was wet I had to sit and show her pictures in books, or help her play with her toys.

I went at 9 o'clock in the morning and stayed until four in the afternoon at first. But after a bit the woman said that I might as well do a few things round the house while I was there. So I used to dust and clean and wash floors, and help in the kitchen at meal times, and carry trays upstairs to the people in their rooms. Eventually it was getting to be seven o'clock, and sometimes even eight o'clock at night, before I was getting away. My wages was fifteen shillings a week, and my dad said I was to tell them they'd got to put my money up if I was working such long hours. So they put me up to a pound, but I had to go in on Saturdays and Sundays for a few hours as well, otherwise they couldn't afford it, they said.

That went on for nearly two years. Then one day when I was fourteen—though they thought I was sixteen, of course—they said they were going to have a bit of a holiday abroad somewhere, and they'd let the number of patients run down to nothing so they could get away. But when the time came there were still three of them there that needed looking after. The woman and her husband told me I'd have to go there and live in the house for three weeks while they was away with the children, but they'd make it up to me when they came back, and perhaps even take me with them the next year when they went abroad. So I moved in to the house for three weeks. I had to get up at six every morning, do all the preparing of meals and serving and cleaning and bed-making and everything for these three old people, it was horrible.

As soon as the woman came back I said I was leaving, I didn't care what; and that was the end of that. My dad backed me up about it and said he'd get me another job, but of course there wasn't much work in the village.

I was hanging around at home for a bit, and then suddenly my sister Irene left, she went off to London with a feller she'd met somewhere, at a dance I think, in one of the holiday places. So that meant I had to stay at home and look after the others. I didn't like it, but there was no one else to do it, I was the oldest girl at home then, apart from my other sister Jean, who was working in a pickle factory in the next village.

Things were very dull all day at home, and although I liked my other brothers and sisters, the one I was most fondest of was Irene, and I missed her terrible. She never wrote to us and we didn't hear anything about her, and me dad didn't talk about her at all, I think her going-off had really upset him. Now and again there'd be a dance in one of the villages round about, and I used to go to some of them with one of my younger sisters or another girl or two from our village. A few of the local boys would make up a group that played guitars and that, and there'd be a record player, it was all a very scratched up affair, know what I mean?

Well one night I went to one of these dances, I think it was on a Friday, it was summer and very hot and after the dance one of the boys who was bass guitarist in the group, he asked me if he could walk me home, and on the way he asked me would I go in the woods with him. I quite liked him and I thought it was real big romance. We went in the woods and started petting and that, and then it got really going and well, that was it. It didn't half hurt, too, and I thought Well it's all cracked-up far better than what it is when you actually do it, know what I mean? You live and learn, don't you?

As far as I was concerned, that was all there was to

it: it just happened the once, and that was the end of it. The boy can't have been all that keen either, because I never went out with him again, I saw him at the dances now and again but he just sort of said 'Hello' and left it like that, the same as I did.

A couple of months went by, and I knew enough from what Irene had used to tell me that it'd happened first time; there I was, I was pregnant. I was real scared stiff, I can tell you, I didn't know what to do or who to talk to or anything. I knew me dad would kill me if he found out, and I was really terrified. The weeks went by and I got really like I felt I wanted to die, I was sick and I went off me food. I used to lie in bed at night trembling all over from head to foot wondering what to do.

It was no use telling the boy I was pregnant by, either—he was TB, and he'd gone off to a sanatorium somewhere, so there'd be nothing he could do about it.

I was sure everyone would be able to tell, just by looking at me, what was happening: I was getting fatter and fatter, and I was quite sure me dad was beginning to suspect, because he seemed so cross and moody all the time.

Then suddenly one day he was all smiles, he called us all in the kitchen on a Saturday afternoon, and he said there'd been a letter from Irene come, and he read it out to us all. She was living in London and she'd got married and she was very happy and she'd got a lovely little girl, and she was hoping that the next summer she and her husband would come for their holidays to see us.

When he'd gone out to the pub that night with mum, and all the other kids was put to bed, I went through the pockets of his jacket that was hanging on the back of the kitchen door, and I found Irene's letter, and took it and copied out the address in London that she'd written from, and then put it back in his jacket.

I waited another week until I'd got enough for the railway fare out of the housekeeping money that dad gave me, and then I told a neighbour I was going to go to Penzance for the day to do some shopping ready for Christmas, and would she keep an eye on the kids for me for the day. She said she would, so I went down to the station just as I was—no luggage, no extra clothes, nothing—and I got on the train for London.

When I got there and come out of Paddington station late at night, my life, I was even more scared than I'd been if I'd stayed at home. I'd no idea London was so big and so noisy and with so many people in it; and I'd no idea at all of how to find the address where my sister was living at.

I was wandering about on the station when a policeman came up to me and asked me where I was going, so I told him I'd come up to have a holiday with my sister, and I showed him the address I'd written down on the paper. 'Oh' he said, 'that's right over the East End, it's no sort of place for a young girl like you to be wandering about this time of night,' and he gave me an address to go to, some sort of hostel place I think it was, where he said I'd be able to sleep for the night and then go over to me sister's in the morning.

So I said Yes, ta, right, thanks very much, and the moment I'd got out of his sight I went and asked a taxi-driver on the rank outside the station if he'd take me to my sister's address, and I said she'd pay him when we got there. He give me a look and then he said 'All right, hop in' and off we went. I don't know whether he believed me at first about me sister or not, because he kept trying to chat me up all the time he was driving me over to the East End, you know trying to get fresh and that. But I wasn't having any, I just Yes'd and No'd him and no more, till he pulls up outside the buildings where my sister lived.

It was one of these places like here where we are now. It's not easy to find out the exact flat where someone is, if you've never been before, know what I mean? So I was going round knocking at doors and ringing on bells and getting nowhere, until suddenly just by absolute luck there I am banging on a door to ask where Number whatever-it-was is, and it opens and there's Irene standing in her nightdress with her hair in curlers. She just looks at me and says 'Oh hello love, come in, what's up then, you're going to have a baby aren't you? Ah well, you'd best sit down and I'll make you a nice cup of tea, and then you'd better get a good night's rest on that couch there, and we'll talk all about it in the morning, all right?'

I didn't have to say anything, I just knew everything'd be right once I'd got to Irene's; I knew she'd take me in and look after me and straighten everything out for me, and I didn't need to worry no more. I did what she said, just lay down on the couch and went to sleep and left it to her.

The next morning I told her all about everything, how it had happened and that, and she went off out and sent a telegram to me mum and dad to tell them I was with her and was all right. Later in the day a telegram come back to say she's to send me straight home again, so Irene fixes-up to go out and telephone them in the evening at one of the village shops where they can go so she can talk to them. She tells them I'm perfectly all right but I'm not coming back for a bit, I'm staying right where I am with her, and she's looking after me.

The feller she's living with isn't the same one she

came to London with, it's another one. But he was very nice about me coming there, and said I could stay as long as I liked, even though they'd only got just the two rooms like here.

Irene was nine years older than me, and as far as I was concerned she knew everything and I did whatever she said was best. When she told me the best thing would be to have the baby adopted as soon as it was born, and she knew a place where it could be arranged, I said it was all right with me and we went along together to these offices. She told the woman there all about me, how young I was and how I'd no place to keep it when it was born, and all the rest of it. The woman was very nice, she said they'd take it a few days after it was born, first of all they'd foster it and then they'd get it adopted.

Then we went down the clinic at the London Hospital, and Irene booked me in there, arranged for me to have a bed when the time came, and that was it. She told me all about what it would be like having it, how I'd just get one pain in me back and then it'd be over, and then in a few days they'd come for the baby and I'd have no more to worry about. She'd had two, she said: the first one had been adopted, and the second was with foster-parents and probably it'd be adopted soon as well.

By then I was five months, so I just lived quietly at Irene's waiting for the time to come. Her husband, or boy friend rather, was very good to me: his name was Stan, and he seemed to have quite a bit of money to throw about, and was keen on having a good time, going dancing and out to clubs a lot.

One afternoon I was in the flat on my own and there was a knock at the door and I opened it, and there was two fellers in raincoats asking for him. I said he was out, so with that they just walks in and starts picking things up and looking at them, opening drawers and shutting them, trying to look in the bedroom and that sort of thing. I got really scared, I said 'What's it all about, what's going on?' but they just grinned and said how long would Stan be, and was I his bird?

In the middle of it all Irene comes back, and as soon as she sets eyes on them she starts yelling and screaming at them and telling them to eff off out of it. 'All right, all right' says one of them, 'calm down now, will you, just tell Stan we'd like to see him down the road when he gets back.'

Irene throws them out, and she still goes on swearing and cursing about them after they've gone, calling them every name under the sun. 'Bleeding coppers' is about the only one I can repeat.

This is all new to me, of course, my idea of a policeman's a fat man on a bike, like we had back at home in our village with a helmet on. When Stan came in Irene starts off again about them, effing and blinding, and he said all right, he'd go and see them. Course he didn't come back that night, and Irene had to go down to the police station and bail him out the next morning. I went down with her.

In the next couple of months the C.I.D. came four or five times asking about things. I used to panic the first time or two, I was frightened of them, but Irene wasn't, she was well used to it, and could swear better than any man could at them. Then of course one night after they come asking for Stan to go down to the station he didn't come back and they wouldn't let him out on bail either. That was it, he was away in the nick for eighteen months.

I don't think he'd been gone more than a few days when another feller moved in with Irene. He was just the same, the C.I.D. kept coming round after him too.

One of the women who lived in another of the flats, she had a couple of kids at primary school, and I used to walk up to the school some afternoons to collect them for her. One day when I got up there it was raining and I was too early, so I went inside the door to wait. Right inside there was a little sort of cloakroom with the teachers' hats and coats hanging-up, so I nipped in and had a quick go through all the pockets. I was right out of luck until I come to the last one, a woman's coat with a purse in it, and inside there was five one pound notes. I had them very quick, didn't I, and then just as I was coming out of the cloakroom again one of the teachers, a man, came along the corridor. I told him I was just looking for the toilet and he gave me a look, but he didn't say much, and I collected the kids and went home.

A couple of days later, bang bang at the door of the flat. When I opened it I started straight off like Irene at the two fellers in macs there, telling them to clear off because the bloke they was looking for wasn't in. 'It's not him this time, Carol' one of them says, 'it's you, darlin'—come on, down to the station wiv us in our nice big car.'

When they get me down there they're going on and on about this money in the purse in the cloakroom, how somebody described me and actually saw me with my hand in the coat pocket through the window, and all the rest of it. I'm just sitting there like Irene told me, saying 'I don't know what you're on about, I never went near the cloakroom, so how could I have been seen in it?' I kept hoping Irene'd know where I was, and come down and help me out, but she didn't. I was so big with the baby I was carrying, and so uncomfortable, and so tired, that when one of them said 'Now come on Carol, fivers can easy be traced you know, and we've got the number of it'—I fell straight into it, I said, 'It wasn't a fiver, it was five ones . . .' and that was it.

They had me up in the court the next morning, and the magistrate took one look at me and put me straight on probation. As I'm going out of the court with Irene, one of the plain-clothes men grins at me. 'Be seeing you back again soon, Carol' he says, the cheeky sod.

Irene said probation was nothing to worry about so long as I didn't do anything else stupid; and then a few days after that my pains started and in I went to the London to have my baby. It all happened just like she'd said: a bit of a pain in the back, and then it was over, and there it was, I had a little boy.

He was really smashing, ever so lively he was. I called him James after my elder brother Jimmy, and Robert after my dad. Irene went really potty over him, and the chap she was living with said I was to bring him back to the flat with me, I wasn't to let him be adopted. The next night Irene and him turned up with a whole pile of new clothes for it, because thinking it would be adopted I'd bought nothing at all, you see.

Then I had a long letter from my mum and dad. Irene had 'phoned them up and told them about the baby, and how lovely he was, and what we'd decided to call him—and mum and dad wrote that I was to go home to them the very day I come out of hospital, with the baby, and they sent the fare and some money for clothes. And they said if I didn't fetch him home, they'd come to London to get us themselves on the very next train.

Irene said I ought to go, so that's what I did. I wasn't frightened no more, not after their letter, and when I got back home they made such a fuss of me and the baby, I could hardly believe it. Dad bought a pram for him, and mum said if I ever wanted to go out in the evenings and enjoy myself I could, she'd be there to look after baby, he'd be quite all right. She seemed to take him right over, you know how I mean, from the very moment I got there, and after a week or two he just didn't seem to be like my baby at all.

'He fits in just nice' she used to say, meaning he was only a couple of years younger than her youngest one, and she used to talk about 'his brothers and sisters' when she meant mine. It wasn't that she was unkind or anything like that, I think my mum just loves children, and she was never really happy unless there was a new baby in the house. He was very good, no trouble about feeding or sleeping, and she really loved having him. He's been there with her ever since. My mum would never part with him now. He thinks I'm his sister. She brought him up to London once, she and my dad came up for a few days with him: he didn't like it here at all, he kept saying 'Want to go home, want to go home.'

Well as I say, mum took him over as soon as I went home. But going out to enjoy myself in the evenings down there seemed—oh, I don't know, just pointless and dull and boring, no life at all, really deadly after round here, know what I mean? I'd only been away a few months, but everything had changed so much, all the people were different, they were almost like strangers, nothing was going on, it was terrible, really terrible.

I wrote to Irene, I said I can't stand it, I want to come back, but I daren't ask my dad for the fare, he'd never give it to me, could you send me a ticket? And of course she did.

She'd moved to a new place, just round the corner

from here, with a new feller, because the other one he'd gone in the nick too. She was working in a little tailoring factory, and she got me in there too, and started me off on learning machining and that. Altogether I worked at it for about ten months, but I didn't enjoy it, not the last part of it, anyway, because Irene had left by then.

I used to knock around with different boys, spend the evenings going in the caffs and the clubs with them, and with my sister and her feller, I went out a lot with them. One night there was this boy in one of the clubs, I knew him from seeing him around, his name was Pete Jones, he come up to me and he said 'You look tired, Carol.' 'I am tired' I said. 'I've been out dancing the last four nights, I feel really wore out.' 'Here you are then' he says. 'Try a couple of these, they'll brighten you up' and he gave me these white pills, they looked like Anadin. I was having a drink at the time, smoking and talking with some girls and fellers, so I just swallowed them down. Before I knew where I was, it seemed I just couldn't stop talking—I was going on and on, feeling really terrific, I was dancing again, I felt marvellous.

I went over to this boy Pete and asked him what they were that he'd given me, he said they were called Preludin, so I said, 'Well give us a couple more, will you, they're terrific.' He said they cost him a bob each, and I said that was all right, I'd have ten bob's worth, so he give me ten.

I stayed up all night in the club, taking these pills every hour or so, and I'd never enjoyed myself so much in all my life, I felt on top of the world, as though I could go on dancing and talking and laughing for ever and ever, just listening to records on the juke box and smoking and drinking coffee.

But the next morning when the pills had all gone and their effect had wore off—it was just like I wanted to fall down dead, honest—you know, all the stuffing gone out of your body, your mouth dry, your head spinning, your heart going a mile a minute, oh you feel shocking, terrible, I can't describe it. All I wanted to do was to go to bed and sleep and sleep. I went back to my sister's and of course the door was shut, she was out at work. I went wandering round the cafés, looking for somewhere where I could put my head down.

When I finally got into one that was nice and quiet, the feller behind the counter who I knew, he said to me 'What's up, Carol, you look as though you're dying?' I said 'I feel it too' and I told him about these pills I'd took the night before. I said 'I've either got to get some more, or I've got to find somewhere where I can lie down and sleep till tomorrow.' 'Why don't you go down the chemist's at the bottom?' he said, 'Tell him how you're fixed, he'll probably let you have a few.'

'Yes,' I said, 'thanks, I never thought of that.' I went down the road into this chemist's and asked him if he'd got any of these Preludin pills, and he said he had, but he couldn't give me any because they were on prescription. 'Look' I said, 'I don't care how much I have to pay for them, just give me a few to keep me going till my sister gets back and I can go home and get to sleep, will you?' So he says 'Well, they're expensive, they're sixpence each off prescription.' Even though I felt terrible I had to laugh, I couldn't help it, I said 'My God, I never thought they'd be that much, I'll have a couple of dozen.' He gave me a real funny look as though he couldn't see what there was to laugh about, but all the same he handed them over, and I'd got six in my mouth and swallowed them down before I was even out of his shop.

Course that set me going again, didn't it, so by the time my sister was home I was back down the club singing and dancing with the juke box and feeling marvellous again. All through that night I go again—till the following morning and there I am staggering about feeling terrible once more, and back into the chemist's shop pleading with him for another ten bob's worth of pills. So he starts off at me about how it's against the law for him to let me have them and all that rubbish, but it doesn't stop him handing them over and making a bit for himself.

Well, that's how it went on. I more or less stopped going to work altogether, and I moved out of my sister's place into a room with that boy Pete Jones I was telling you about, who could get the pills himself when I couldn't. I'd go on for weeks at a time, hardly going to bed at all, just sitting around in the cafés during the day and the clubs at night, listening to records and taking pills one after another, more and more at a time until I was eating them, really eating them, by the handful. I used to go into the chemist and buy them off-of him first of all by the pound's worth, then two or three pounds' worth, then finally at seven pound ten for a big bottle of two hundred and fifty. A sweet thing he was making out of it too, I reckon: I found out a bit ago the trade price he was buying them at was fifty-five shillings.

Everybody in the cafés and clubs used to call me 'Carol The Pill', and if anybody got any they always come and sold them to me. Sometimes I used to think, What'll I do if they suddenly stop manufacturing them, I'll die, won't I? Well, I thought, I'll go onto something else if that happens, I'll have to: and in the meantime I'd better make sure I've got plenty to be going on with.

I don't think Pete was quite as bad about them as I was, but the fact that he was on them too kept us together, we sort of shared each other's supplies. When you get onto the pills and you get really blocked-up, you're happy, you've no worries, you just sit and drink and talk and dance all day and all night. You don't want any sex, nothing like that, you lose interest in it and you can't stand anyone touching you. That's why Pete was the ideal person for me to be living with, we neither of us touched each other hardly at all. If anyone did try to get fresh with me in a club or anywhere, I'd just stand straight up and whack them and tell them to keep their hands off-of me: one time I gave a feller a terrific smack in the eye with my fist and then broke a Coke bottle over his head. Oh yes, I was real wild and I'd fight with anybody, girls or fellers, I wasn't scared of no one. You don't care about nothing and nobody when you're like that, especially if you're strong like me.

Pete was always dead jealous of anyone else talking to me. He used to carry a knife around with him, and one night he saw me outside a club talking to a feller, and he came up and started going off about it at us. I told him to shut his so-and-so mouth, and then I whacked him one and walked off. He came running after me and he hit me, I felt it in my side, I thought he'd kicked me, and I shouted at him 'You shouldn't have done that, should you?' and I really set about him. I think I'd have killed him, but all of a sudden I felt my skirt was wet at the top, and I put my hand down to my side and found I was all over blood, because Pete had stabbed me.

He got up from the ground where I'd knocked him down, and rushed off to get a taxi to take me down the hospital. When I got there, the doctor came and he said I'd have to be stitched-up and stay in the hospital till they found out whether I'd been damaged inside. He said 'How did it happen?' and I said I'd been at home and I'd went to sit down in this arm-chair, and this knife which had been dropped down the side of it had stuck right into me. He said well that was funny, because the wound went straight into me sideways, not upwards, and I was all bruised as well. So I said I'd always been the sort who bruised very easy, and I'd probably banged myself on the chair when I jumped up —and now would he just do what was needed to stitch me up, and I'd come back the next day to tell him if I didn't feel better. So he gave me a look and let me go.

I felt terrible the next few days, and stayed in bed in the room. Pete looked after me until I went back to have the stitches out, and after a bit I was back in the cafés again. The ball was still rolling, I swallowed the pills and smoked and drank milk, tons of milk,* and ate egg sandwiches, and that was how I lived. I was very happy, happy all the time, laughing and dancing, and my only worry was where I was going to get money from to keep on buying the pills.

I did a bit of rolling now and again, working with some of the girls round the cafés who were prostitutes. That's where she takes the feller back to her place and gets him to undress like in here, the living room, then takes him in there, the bedroom. While they're in there, I'm hiding over there, say behind the settee, and I go through his clothes and take everything that has any value at all—money, watch, wallet, whatever he has— and then clear out. Usually he doesn't find out till he's gone, but even if he does, well he's never seen me and

---

* (Dr. Derek Miller comments at length in his book on the psychosocial treatment of delinquent youth, *Growth To Freedom*, (Tavistock, 1964) how "Under stress late adolescents consume large quantities of milk." T.P.).

it can't be the other girl, can it, since she's been with him all the time, see what I mean?

But that was always a bit uncertain, really, you never knew how much you were going to get in a day, and you always had to share with the girl doing the prostituting. Prostitutes aren't thieves themselves usually, and thieves aren't prostitutes, but sometimes they work together. It's very rare you'll find a girl doing both. Some of the old ooers (*whores*) do, they'll thieve off-of anyone and jump in bed with anyone, they're right slags a lot of them, do anything. But as I say, with a young girl you're either a thief or a street-girl usually, and the two aren't mixed.

Pete was in with a mob used to do a few jobs down in Surrey, the big houses out there. I'd go with them and sit in the car to keep watch while they screwed two or three places in a night. We'd get all sorts of mixed gear —furs, jewellery, gold cigarette boxes, whisky—but it all had to be fenced and then divided up, so many shares for you, so many for me. You had to keep at it pretty steady to make a living—and when you were on the pills very heavy like I was, there was always the constant need of money to buy them with.

The C.I.D. were always coming round our place looking for stuff, but Pete and me never kept anything nicked there, it'd be stupid, wouldn't it? They took me in one time on an I.D. parade, some woman whose house had been done said she'd seen a girl sitting outside in a car, a girl with long dark hair. The Law said to me 'We're putting you up with a lot of other girls, you can stand anywhere you like in the line before we let this woman in, and see if she identifies you.'

And then when they gets me inside, there's these six girls, every one of them a blonde, all office girls in smart coats and handbags and that—and me they've just pulled in out of the café down the street, all grubby! Anyway, they was unlucky that time, because this old bag said she couldn't pick anyone out. I gave her a real dark look, you know, when she come down the line, much as to say to her 'Go on, you pick me out and I'll kick your throat in.'

Like I said, you don't care, when you're on the pills, what you look like or what you do, and you can get very abusive too. I was effin and blindin' at the Law when I went out of the station for taking me in, but somehow I knew it wasn't going to be long now before they'd really got something to hang on me.

It was only a few days later, and I was walking down the street with Pete and a couple of other boys and another girl, and we were all a bit noisy and that, when an Indian bloke said something to me, started getting fresh and that, so I whacked him one. He hit me one back, then Pete and the boys turned round and went for him and knocked him down and gave him a kicking.

As he fell his wrist-watch strap broke and his watch fell off, so I picked it up and went off with it. That afternoon I'm sitting in the café, and in comes the Law. 'Right Carol' they say, 'Come on.' 'Oh leave me alone, I said 'Not again, haven't you got nothing better to do?'

Down the station we go and there's this Indian. 'That's her!' he says, 'she's the one took my watch.' Well of course I've got it on, haven't I, so that's it. 'We've got you darling' the Law bloke says. 'You're finished now, ain't yer, Carol?' I'm remanded in custody at the magistrates' court, charged with robbery with violence. There's an old woman gives evidence to say she saw me attack this Indian and take his watch. When she comes past the dock, I climbed over and took a punch at her, cursing her like mad I was, till they dragged me downstairs. They picked up Pete and the others a day or two later, and eventually we're all charged together.

On remand I was put in Holloway, and of course the pills started wearing off and it was terrible. I was crying and yelling, getting really depressed, telling Irene when she came to see me that she'd got to get me out, or send me in some pills, throw them over the wall to me, anything. But gradually I got over it and calmed down.

We were up at the Old Bailey on this charge. The judge went quite heavy on the other boys, but Pete only got twelve months. Me, the judge said, I'd got to go to Borstal for a period of training between 6 months and 2 years.

Back I go straight to Holloway, and they put me to work in the laundry. Then one morning after a few weeks an officer come in my cell, she says 'Come with me' and takes me off down the hospital where she weighs me, looks in my hair and everything, then takes me to have a bath and after that puts me up in front of the Wing Governor. 'Carol' she says, 'we're sending you on to an open Borstal tomorrow. It's a great chance for you, would you like to go?'

I thought Well, if it's open that means all I'll have to do is walk out, so I said 'Yes.' The next day they take me out to this place, it's like a big house in the country, and the screws don't wear uniform. But they've got all sorts of terrible rules and regulations. You're paid two shillings a week to start with, and they knock money off for everything—a penny if you're late for work by one minute, tuppence for two minutes, and so on like that. Worst thing of all is they take it off for bad language. The first afternoon I was there a screw said to me 'Carol, go and sweep up the dining-room, will you?'

and I said 'Oh go and shag yourself' and she said 'Right that's a shilling off your wages.'

Well I mean it's impossible, isn't it? And they're all the time on to you about being a good girl, turning over a new leaf, all that lark. My sister and her feller came down to see me at the week-end and I told them I was going to have it away, they said to give the place a try, but I told them it was useless, I was never going to have any money there at all.

Another girl, Sheila, she felt the same way as me, and a couple of nights later we went; out through the kitchen when everyone was in bed, through the vegetable garden, over the wall into the cemetery, and out onto the road and started to walk. Every time we saw the lights of a car coming we chucked ourselves down in the ditch at the side of the road. Eventually we came to a transport café. We hung about outside until a driver came out, and we asked him if he'd give us a lift to London. He said he was going the other way himself, but he pointed out a tanker and said if we waited a bit, the driver of that would be coming out, and he was going to London. We got up in his cab to wait for him, and when he arrived we said he was going to take us up to Town, wasn't he? He sort of sighed and said 'Yes all right.' He didn't talk much on the journey, gave us a cigarette now and again, and then he dropped us off somewhere down near the docks.

We must have looked a right pair walking about round there in the middle of the night; it's a wonder the Law didn't spot us. We'd got these horrible blue gaberdine school macs and heavy black shoes and brown ankle socks. Sheila wanted to get over to Bayswater where she knew someone, but she didn't know how to do it, so she said she was going to give herself up. I said I wasn't, not after I'd got all that way, I said if they wanted me they'd have to catch me, so we separated and I made my own way through the streets until I got out on to the Commercial Road, and could find my way to Irene's.

I slept on her couch for what was left of the night, and in the morning she said I'd have to move on to some friends, because the Law was sure to come looking for me. Next day I went down one of the clubs and hung about there, and I met a girl I knew and went back to her place for the night. It was only two weeks to Christmas, and I thought I'd try and get some money and get back to Cornwall. Me and this other girl decided to go thieving for it. We went into a shop and tried to nick a coat, and got caught straight off for it. They sent for the police, and they came and took us down to the station.

When we got inside a woman police sergeant says to me 'Here, aren't you Carol Dean?' 'Not me' I says, 'She's in Borstal,' and right that minute a C.I.D. bloke comes walking through. 'Hello Carol' he says, 'Merry Christmas'—so that was it, I'm straight back in Holloway.

I ask to see the Wing Governor straight away, and when I come up in front of her I says can I go back to the open Borstal because I liked it and thought it was doing me good. Eff off, she says, or a Borstal Governor's equivalent, and I have to stay in Holloway for nearly all the rest of my time, back working in the laundry again. I was on a machine with two old lags, one doing twelve years and the other eight, and a right dreary pair they was too.

It was hard work in Holloway, boring, and a lot of time locked up in your cell, but it went quite quick and I preferred it to that open place; the screws were much better, they weren't always on at you about reform.

You could just do your time and get on with it. I was there nearly fifteen months altogether, then I was sent to another Borstal, what they call a semi-secure one, where I did my last three months before they let me out.

It was rotten when I came out at first, it takes a week or ten days before the feeling of being in prison completely wears off. I didn't want to go out the first day or two, or work, or anything. I was on licence, of course, and they'd told me I was going to be taken back again if I got into any trouble, so I had to go easy. I got a job as a petrol pump attendant at a garage for a bit, and stayed living with my sister. But of course having a record, the police were on to me about everything, taking me in for questioning all the time, really pushing me, know what I mean?

When that prostitute was found murdered on a bomb-site, they knew she was a friend of mine, so down they come, when did I last see her, who was her friends, who was her boy friend, was I a street-girl too, who was my boy friend, was he a ponce,—shocking they were, the things they asked me had nothing to do with it at all. They're not too particular about twisting your arm and that, either, and giving you a thump if they think you're not telling them what they want to know. Their attitude is that you must be guilty of something, if they can only find what it is. They've slacked-off a bit now because my licence is over, and they seem to be leaving me alone, but I don't expect it'll last, they'll be round after me or my boy friend before long, I suppose.

If I'm here, that is. But I might not be, I may be with someone else, I don't seem able to stick with one chap for long. That's why I'd be frightened ever to get married. I can be with someone a long time, and then all of a sudden I've gone right off-of them in an hour, that's it, it's finished, I just don't like them anymore, I'm real fed up with them and want to go back and live with Irene for a bit. There's one feller now I know, brings me bits of jewellery and things he's got off different houses he's done, he's always asking me to marry him, but I just can't stand him. Everything he brings me, I sell it or pawn it, I don't know why he doesn't give up. After all there's nothing special about me, there's lots of girls round here he could have who are no different from me in any way, they're just ordinary thieves like I am, that's all.

Funny, isn't it, the way some men are like that, they kind of fix on something or somebody they want, and nothing else'll do? But I don't want to belong to anybody like that, at least not for years and years yet. I just want to go on like I am, young and happy and healthy and enjoying myself and having a bit of fun. I can look after myself; and if there's anything I really want I can always go out and thieve it. I've had a bit of bad luck going to prison, but I don't think it's done me all that much harm really, do you?

DIANE RICHARDS

FORGERY

AGE: *24*
NUMBER OF CONVICTIONS: *4*
TOTAL TIME SPENT IN PRISON: *3 years 3 months*

II

Diane Richards

The summer was settled and warm, with the days one after another dissolving into long evenings that were breathless and still. Each night as darkness slowly came the noises of cars and playing children through the open window from the street below grew fewer and faded, and it seemed sometimes the only sound left in the world was the nervous click-clicking of the cigarette lighter she held in her fingers, the only light the on-and-off flicker of its flame illuminating momentarily and repeatedly her pretty face in the dark.

Most nights she curled in an armchair, with her legs pulled-up underneath her; tiny, neatly proportioned like a doll, four feet ten and a half inches high, weighing just over a hundred pounds. Little hands, lacquered nails, cheap bejewelled sandals on small bare feet; brown stretch nylon trews and a thin yellow sweater, showing underneath it the shadow of her black bra. Pale blue eyes in a small-featured face, long hair swept round and up and piled high in an extravagant back-combed and blonded crescendo on top of her head.

In the centre of the room a large bed with a purple candlewick bedspread, and a toy dog placed carefully in the middle; over in one corner a wooden airing-rack with lingerie on it—a blue slip, frilly red nylon briefs, a black girdle, stockings. A crinoline-doll lamp on the dressing-table, an alarm-clock, three jars of make-up and a bottle of perfume. An empty wine bottle on the chest of drawers, two postcards, a pair of white gloves, an unopened box of Callard and Bowser's nougat. On top of the shilling-in-the-slot television-set a packet of cigarettes, a light blue Dinky-Toy Mini-Minor, some hairpins ... The marks of her person and personality scarcely impinged on the incurable emptiness of the huge furnished room with its large spaces of shiny grey lino, its faded brown curtains at the window, the cracked mirror over the fireplace and the unshaded light-bulb hanging from the ceiling. She looked lost in it, marooned, the transience of her presence epitomised by her suitcase which lay resting ready to hand on the cupboard near the door; she was too small for it, a lost and lonely little Irish girl ...

Sometimes when everything weighed desperately down on her, she would get up and walk aimlessly about, puffing at her cigarette, flip-flopping in her sandals round the room talking, forgetting anyone else was there, on and on out of her small and thin-lipped mouth coming the hard harsh words for half an hour, or an hour, with no prompting needed at all. At first it was never about anything else but prison: the place she had left months ago—but was living in still.

* * * * * * *

In prison you live in the past, you see Tony, thinking of things that happened to you when you were outside. They happened to you in the past, and you go on and on thinking about them, and sure you never think about the future at all. Prison's a world on its own, it's the only real world there is; you know that some day you're going to get out of it, but it's so far away it isn't worth thinking about.

I'd got three years last time, so I knew it'd have to be two inside at very least, I'd have to be in there for two years whatever happened, it couldn't be less than that. So I just forgot the outside, I got on with doing it, it was me life, my whole life it was, for all of two years.

Then they came one morning and they said 'Right now Diane, come on now you're going out in a couple of weeks.' And before you've really woken up to it—Bang, it's there, that's it, you're out. Suddenly it falls on you, it's terrible, it's dreadful, it really is, everything's absolutely upside down, you can't take it and you're terrified.

This time I just didn't want to come out. You've been away all that long time, you see, and you say to yourself God, what's happened to me, what are the changes in me, I must look so different from other people now, they're bound to know where I've come from, they must. On the 'bus, going into shops, trying to get a room: they look at you, and you think—they can tell, they'll say something to me any minute, they'll tell me they don't want to know me and to go away.

Early on I went to the After-Care, I couldn't stand it, I said 'Please send me back inside, I want to go back, I'm on licence to you, recall me off my licence, anything.' They said 'Cheer up, it'll wear off, everyone feels like that at first, Diane.' They're wrong...

Last August Bank Holiday all the girls on my landing we all went mad fighting and screaming and carrying on. There was me and Sylvia and Margaret and Joan: we decided to barricade, we all got in my cell and we piled everything up against the door and then yelled at the screws to come and try to get us out. One of them they call Big Davies, she came along and started pushing at the door; she got her shoulder in and then she got her head in, and I caught her with the edge of the door in her neck, jammed her against the upright so she couldn't get either in or out. We were all going mad, then some more screws came along and they all got behind Big Davies and shoved, and suddenly I let go of the door and they all came tumbling in on top of us. I got sent down on punishment and put on Rule 36 for a month; seven o'clock in the morning they come and take your bed out, all you've got is a chair to sit on all day by yourself and they give you mailbags to sew. They kept coming down to see me, the screws, telling me to be a good girl. They weren't nasty about it; there are some quite decent screws really, just do their job, most of them, they don't hold things against you. Some of them even bring you fags and pieces of chocolate and things when you're on punishment.

Another time we cut the wires of the Wing telephone one night. That was really funny, we had a right laugh then, they couldn't find out who'd done it or how it'd been done, everyone was going crazy about it. I had a big pink bow in me hair I'd got off a chocolate box one of the girls had had for her birthday, and I was rushing up and down the Wing dancing about with it on and shouting at everybody, saying we'd all have to shout now there was no telephone . . .

Stupid. We were all laughing though, it seemed the funniest thing out at the time. Sounds silly doesn't it to say we had some real good times in there, but it's true, we really did, everyone was friends, we had some good laughs together, lots of fun, all the girls they were so nice to me, they were so good.

I felt terrible leaving it all behind you know, Tony, I did. I never thought the day'd come when I'd cry because I was leaving a prison, but I did cry that day, I cried because they were all my friends I was leaving there, and I was coming out just to be on my own.

Free, being free, it just means being free to be lonely that's all. It's terrible this time when I've come out, everything seems against me, nothing goes right; it's because I didn't want to come out. Why should I, just to be alone? But that's it, it's over, I'm out. Here I am. Here I am, and look at me—trying not to cry at thinking back about when I was in prison. Look at me, thinking about prison and trying not to cry.

* * * * * * *

1940 I was born, December 1940, in Dublin. I've got one brother, four years older than me, he's in Birmingham, I haven't seen him for years, he's with me father I think, working there.

We lived in a flat in a house in a square near the South Circular Road, Dublin; my father was a bulldozer driver, worked on building sites and that. He drank a lot. My mother stayed at home and looked after me and my brother Liam. She had brown eyes, lovely brown eyes, and long wavy brown hair, so long and wavy. You know those old-fashioned perms with waves in— just like that. I used to think she had hair like Jesus must have had. She was a bit taller than I am now, but not much, and very good to everybody, everybody loved her; I can remember on Sundays she used to send me up to me grandpa with a packet of cigarettes and one of those little bottles of whisky, and she used to say 'Don't let your grandma see it, will you now

Diane?' She used to buy sweets for Liam and me, a bag each for us, and she dressed us so nicely and looked after us, and she got Post Office savings books for the two of us, and put a bit of money in every week that she'd saved for us out of the housekeeping.

Then she took ill, very sudden it was, I can remember her lying in bed, and us all having to be quiet because she was so ill. She died very quick, she was only thirty-five. There was the funeral and everybody drinking like they do in Ireland, the flat full of people and all the noise. I remember my father shouting and reeling about, and then stopping and looking at me with his eyes all red, and shouting 'Well go on, why don't you die too, and I'll buy you a coffin like I bought your mother, eh?'

About six I'd be I suppose, then; maybe he'd had too much because he was trying to drown his sorrows. But I've always hated him, ever since, for that.

He drank more and more after she'd died, he seemed to stop work and just drink. We had to leave the flat, and I went with Liam to stay with one of my aunties. I don't know where my father went, he used to come and see us from time to time and say he'd come to take us out. It was always to the same place, down to the Post Office, where we'd sign the form for drawing money out of our Savings Books and give it to him. It was for our school-books, he used to say. Then he'd buy us a few sweets and take us back to our auntie's. He had about forty pounds from each of us, until it was all gone. Years after, I found my book, just a couple of shillings it had in it, and you could see all those withdrawals from when I was young.

I don't know what my auntie said to him, but we saw less and less of him, until suddenly one day when Liam was fourteen he came and said he was taking him to

England with him to get a job and I never saw either of them no more after that. He liked Liam better than me: he was good at school, and kept himself neat and tidy. Me, I was always dirty, my hair all over the place, like a wild thing I was. I went on going to school on my own, but I didn't like it much, it was a convent school and I was always truanting and getting into trouble for getting dirty or losing my hair-ribbons. My hair was long and I hated it, one day when I was twelve I went to the barber's and got him to cut it all off. Then it was short and I didn't have it pulled about and put in plaits all the time; I liked it better but it still didn't make me behave any more.

I was awful rebellious against everyone, against the school, against the Church, against my auntie. If anybody checked me I used to shout at them 'You wouldn't do that if me mum was alive, she wouldn't have let you.' I didn't want anyone to do anything for me but her; and I knew I couldn't have her, so I just wanted to be left alone.

One day some nuns came to the school from England, from south London somewhere on a visit. They told us all about the war and the air-raids and the bombing, and how their convent had been hit by a bomb and set on fire, and then another bomb had fallen on it and burst all the water pipes and put the fire out again. I thought it was marvellous, miracles dropping out of the sky just like that. I made up my mind that was what I wanted to be, a nun, and go and live in England in this convent.

When I came 14 I told my auntie I wanted to leave school and go in for a nun straight away. She wrote off to the convent in London, but they said they couldn't take me there, I'd have to talk to the priest where I lived.

Then, well you know how it is with kids, time went on and I went to work in a shop that another of my aunties had, a groceries. I was still thinking how I'd like to be a nun one day; but I never got anywhere near it and I thought I was finished, I thought my life was going to go on for years and years with me being just an assistant in a groceries in a side street. But there was two girls I'd got friendly with, sisters, they used to come in the shop sometimes, and one day they said they were going to England to work in a hotel in the Lake District, they'd got a job through an agency, and they said 'Why don't you come with us, Diane?'

I wrote to the hotel they were going to, to see if they had another job going, and they had. I told the people I was seventeen, but really I was only just over 15; then I went to the agency and got my ticket, and that was it, I was ready for off. I went home and told my auntie I was going at the end of the week, I'd got my ticket and I'd got a job to go to, and there was nothing she could do about it. I don't think in a way she was sorry to see me go, I was a responsibility for her and she never knew how to handle me; and perhaps she thought I might go and see my father, too, once I was over in England.

I knew I had to make the break then, and over to England we came, the three of us, Sheelagh and Maureen and me. They'd been over once before to Blackpool for a holiday, but I never had. When I saw the green grass I couldn't believe it, I said 'Oh look, the grass is green!'

Sheelagh and Maureen said 'Well what colour did you think it'd be then?' and I said 'I didn't know they had it in England too, I thought it was only in Ireland.' I'd got the idea England was just one big amusement-park sort of place, something like Blackpool all over, you see, from what they'd told me.

It was lovely up in the Lake District, it was summer, the hotel was a big one and the lady who ran it said to me 'Well I'll be your mother' when I told her my mother was dead. I worked in the kitchen, and Sheelagh and Maureen they were waitresses in the diningroom, and we all shared a room up in the attic, a big room with three beds in it. We stayed there the whole summer, it was really nice. At the end of the season Sheelagh said, 'Well there's no use staying on here, there'll be nothing doing through the winter, come on let's all go to Liverpool to one of the hotels there.'

So off we went, and we spent the winter in Liverpool. I was 16 at Christmas that year, we were still together the three of us, but Sheelagh and Maureen had got themselves boy friends, so I wasn't seeing a lot of them even though we were all working in the same place. At New Year we had a party, all the staff of the hotel, and we were doing a lot of drinking. I got into a really happy frame of mind—you know, not bothering about anything, feeling as though I was floating on air. When one of the little Italian chefs asked me to go up to his bedroom with him I just said 'Yes all right if you like' end off we went upstairs. I let him do what he liked, I wasn't really thinking about anything at all, until I woke up next morning on my own in his bed, with a terrible headache and feeling really—oh, really awful, like I'd done something absolutely terrible.

I was quite sure I was going to have a baby straight away. I told Sheelagh and Maureen about it, and they just laughed, they said 'Well if you can't be good be careful.' This little Italian he seemed to think he owned me after that, he was always either coming to my room or taking me up to his room and getting me on the bed with him. In the spring he left, he went on to another hotel somewhere else. I can't say I was sorry about it. Then Sheelagh said she'd heard of a job going up in Newcastle, would I like to go with her because Maureen didn't want to, she wanted to stay in Liverpool where her feller was. I said all right, and the two of us went up there. After we'd been there a couple of months I found I was pregnant. I worked as long as I could, still as a kitchen-maid, and then I had the baby in the autumn. It was a lovely little thing, a girl. I called her Jean.

At Christmas I wrote to my auntie in Dublin saying I was coming home. I went back with the baby, I told her I was married but my husband had run off and left me, and I had to go back to England to earn the money to keep the baby. My auntie said she'd look after her for me, so back to England I went. As far as I know she's still got her.

When I came back to England, Sheelagh was off one place and Maureen was off another, with different fellers. I went back to Newcastle and got a job up there working on the 'buses. But being so small, it didn't suit me. I met a chap one night in a pub, he seemed quite nice and he said he was going down to Doncaster for the races, would I like to go with him so I said 'Yes if you like.'

He'd done a bit of time for a few bits of things, nothing serious, thieving from unattended vehicles and that sort of stuff. He was called Dick. We stayed in a furnished room in Doncaster a few days, then we moved on to Sheffield where he said some of his mates were living. But when we got there he didn't seem able to find them: he didn't bother looking very hard, I think it was just he wanted to keep moving, never staying long enough in one place to get caught.

Anyway we had this furnished room in Sheffield, and

he used to go out a lot during the day, never saying where he was going or what he was doing, just leaving me to read papers and books all day long in bed. I was always hungry, too. Then I found I was pregnant again, and somehow it seemed to turn me against him, I couldn't stand the sight of him, and we used to have some terrible rows, and after them he'd go out for hours and hours and I'd never know where he was.

One day he did that and I got real fed-up, so I started wandering round the house looking for someone to talk to. I went down into the basement where the landlady lived, to see if she was in: she wasn't, and I was just coming out of her room when I saw her Post Office Savings Book lying on the dresser. I picked it up and looked inside it, and she had about a couple of hundred quid in there. I took it back up to my room, and got a pen and a bit of paper, and had a try at copying her signature that was in the front.

And you know, really, it was quite easy. So off I went to the Post Office straight away. I was going to try and get £3, but the lady in front of me, she asked for £10, so I thought I might as well do the same. The clerk was only a young chap, I gave him a big bright smile when I'd filled the form in and signed it, and I think he was more interested in me than he was in the signature.

It was as easy as that, and there I was with ten quid, I was really delighted. If you know you're skint and it means you're going to be able to eat, and buy a few things, it's surprising what you can do if you try. I went and bought myself some stuff, stockings and make-up and scent and that, then I ran back to the house quick to get the Savings Book back before the landlady came back. But she was already in when I got there, so I thought 'Oh well, I might just as well keep it then, and let's hope she thinks she's lost it if she notices it's gone.'

A few days later I thought I might as well have another ten pounds, so back to the Post Office I go. The clerk gives it me again, but then he says the book's got to go up to Head Office if you draw out over a certain sum within the week, and he gives me an envelope to address so's it can be sent back to me.

That made things a bit awkward, but then I had a bright idea and I said to him 'I'm going to stay with my sister in Doncaster a few days, so it'd best be sent on to me there'—and I put the address where we'd stayed before we came to Sheffield.

When I went back and told Dick he wasn't all that pleased about it, he said he didn't want to go back, but I said with the Savings Book having all that money in it, at least we ought to go and collect it, so back to Doncaster we went. We were only there a day or two, and then it isn't the Savings Book that comes, it's the police of course, so there I was, that was it. Dick was out so they didn't know anything about him, it was just me on my own. It was a Saturday, they kept me in the police station over the week-end, then up to court on the Monday, and I was remanded for a week for enquiries. A week later they took me up to court again and since I was pregnant and hadn't been in trouble before the magistrate said he was going to deal lightly with me and give me a conditional discharge, and that was what he did.

By the time I was let out of course Dick had disappeared and I was on my own. I was a bit worried, knowing I was going to have the baby, but then I had a stroke of luck, I met Maureen again and she said I could go and stay with her and her boy friend in

Bradford while I had the baby. When it was born, Dick heard about it and he turned up to visit me in hospital, but I just didn't fancy him any more, I told him I didn't want no more of him. But he wouldn't give up, he was always hanging around, and eventually we got another room together, in Bradford. I had to leave the baby with Maureen for a while, but she looked after it for me all right, she was very fond of her. She was a lovely kiddie, everybody liked her, she was so good and quiet and no trouble at all. Her name was Anna.

Dick and I were moving around from one furnished place to another, it went on for months and months, with him doing a bit of thieving now and again to keep us going, and sometimes getting-in on some quite big jobs with his mates and we could live in luxury afterwards for a week or two, you know what I mean? I was getting a bit of stuff on H.P. from time to time too, and then selling it again, but only when we were really short. Then one day I had a real big stroke of luck—I picked up a bank book in one of the houses where we were staying—not a Post Office book, but a proper bank one, and it had a hundred pounds in it, which I knew I could get out nearly all at one go.

It was a bit tricky, because of course I didn't know if they'd know in the bank whether I was the right person or not. I didn't dare go in until they were really busy on a Saturday morning, and I had to put on a really big effort for the clerk behind the counter. I didn't draw everything out, only ninety pounds of it.

But the moment I'd done it, I was silly, I said to Dick 'Come on, we've got to go now, right away,' and away we went. I'd have been much more sensible to stay in Bradford and get a job, and pretend I knew nothing about it. It wasn't long before the police had caught up with us again. They were really after Dick, but they took me in as well, and they kept me on remand in custody, just on and on while they made enquiries. Nearly five months it was altogether I was in. Pregnant again I was, and I had the baby in hospital while I was on remand. It was another little girl, she was lovely, I called her Patricia.

This time they put me up in Sessions in front of a Judge who wasn't so easily affected by things. They'd got a lot of charges against me including the H.P. plus some I knew nothing about, and I was found guilty on five counts in all. When this Judge sentenced me, he started saying 'Two years on the first count, two years on the second count, two years on the third count . . .' My head was really swimming, I thought he was swearing my life away and going to give me 10 years altogether. Then right at the end he said 'All to run concurrent with each other', so it was only two years in all. Still it was bad enough, two years and I was only just getting on for 20.

Dick comes down to the cells to see me afterwards and he was crying but I said, 'It's no use crying, it's got to be done and I might as well get on with it.'

They sent me to Manchester at first, and I was allowed to keep Patricia with me for a while. I decided to finish with Dick altogether, so I didn't answer any of his letters or send him visiting orders or anything. Then after a while I got sent to Askham Grange, that's an open prison near York; I was still allowed to keep my baby with me, and Dick kept coming up there to see us, but I wouldn't see him. I let him see the baby but I didn't want any more to do with him myself. I don't know why it was, I'd just gone right off him altogether.

After a bit at Askham they sent me out to work from

the prison every day as a cleaner in a hospital, and I was allowed out at week-ends, I used to go down to Bradford sometimes to see friends. Then after six weeks I was taken off working-out for coming back late one week-end. But it was near the end of my sentence, I hadn't long to wait before it was finished and then they had to let me out, and back to Bradford I went.

A girl who'd been at Askham with me called Sandra, she was living there with some feller or other and I stayed with them for a while. Sandra was on the game, you know, prostituting, and her feller was a bit of a thief. One night I was out with her, we'd been in a pub and when we came out we were standing at the corner waiting for her feller to turn up when a car stops right behind us. Sandra turns round to say something to the driver—and what do you think, it's the Law. 'Right girls,' they said, 'in you get,' and they took us down to the station and charged us with soliciting. I got two years' probation for it, just because I was standing on the street corner with Sandra. She got a fine for it.

Now and again I used to go over to the other side of Bradford to see how my other baby, Anna, was getting on; Maureen still had her, and she was so fond of her, she was like her own two. I said I'd let her go on keeping her for the time being. I said 'I might come back myself any day and take her away, but you can have her for now'—and oh, she was so pleased. The other one, Patricia, various friends looked after from time to time, because I'd got myself in with a chap we'd met one night in a pub. A chap called Jack White, he was in property repairing, working for one of these big firms on contract jobs, he used to go all over the country for them.

He had to go to London on a job for two or three

months, and he asked me would I go with him. I didn't want to at first because I'd heard he was married, but he said he was going to get divorced and then we could get married ourselves. So I arranged for someone to look after Patricia, a lady who'd got several children she was, and she was very fond of her, she was glad to have her, and off we went.

I really thought there was no one like Jack. He was a lot older than me, he was thirty-five, going bald, and real ugly looking—but happy, you know, and a really tough, brave sort of feller. He wanted to take Patricia to London with us, he said I ought to have her with me, and we'd get a flat where we could all live. He'd been a villain all his life, but he'd got to the stage where he wanted to settle down. When we got to London we got a furnished room in Bayswater and everything seemed to be going fine. Then Jack got in a fight one night and he hit some bloke and gave him eight stitches in his forehead, and this bloke's mates were looking for him; the job was finished so he said we might as well go back up north again, so we did, we went to Manchester, which was where Jack really lived, you know, where his home and his wife and kids were. We got a room together and things were a bit hard at first because he'd got no work.

After we'd been there a few days of course I found another Post Office book in one of the other rooms in the house, and I drew the money out in small sums to keep us going. Then Jack got a job, and everything looked as though it was going to turn out alright—until the Law came and picked me up for the Post Office book again.

I was put in Strangeways on remand, and Jack was going crazy trying to get me bail because he'd got no money. He went back to his home and took his radiogram from there and sold it to raise the bail for me to get me out. His wife went potty about it. He told her to mind her own business and he came and got me out, and we went off back to Leeds and Bradford, all over the place. One of his friends lent him a van, and we were touring about, keeping on the move so's the Law wouldn't catch up with us. Then I found I was pregnant again and oh, he was so happy about it, he said 'That settles it Diane, we'll get married now just as soon as I can get my divorce.'

We went back to Manchester so he could talk to his wife about it, and when we got to the house I stayed outside sitting in the van while he went and talked to her. He was in there for ages, so I beeped on the horn to let him know he'd been long enough. And she came out, his wife, like a raving lunatic, swearing and cursing, in front of her own children too. She said 'The police have been here looking for you, and if you don't leave my husband alone you bloody bitch I'll shop you, I swear I will!' I said 'Oh you've got a lovely mouth, haven't you, in front of your children, I must say.' And she said 'You come out of that van you little slut and I'll give you the biggest hiding of your life. I'm telling you' she said, 'if my husband's not back here by seven o'clock to-night I'll shop the pair of you.'

Jack came and got back in the van and we drove off, and he said 'She will, you know, she means it, she'll shop us all right.'

And she did. Eight o'clock that evening the C.I.D. came round to the room we were in: as quick as that. They took me back on remand, and of course there was no bail since I'd jumped it, and then I came up at the Sessions.

I hadn't heard a word from Jack at all, and when I got in court I wasn't bothering about what was going on, I was just looking round for him all the time. The judge said it was time I was pulled-up sharp: 'I'm sending you for three years' Corrective Training' he said, but I wasn't really listening, I was still looking for Jack.

I got moved down to Holloway, and it was three weeks before I heard from him that he was coming down to see me. He came, and he said he'd been to court the day I was there but he couldn't find my name on the list and so he didn't know which court I'd be in, and by the time he found out the case was over. Anyway, he said, I was to apply to the Governor to see if we could get married before the baby was born. 'How can we do that?' I said, 'You're still married.' 'Well' he said, 'I've started the divorce now, and it'll be through in a few weeks and then we'll be married straight away.'

He was off on a job again that was taking him all over the country, and he used to write to me from wherever he was, post-cards and lovely letters, all about the baby that was coming and how he was looking forward to it, and how he was going to have a home and everything ready for me for when I came out. Cambridge he wrote from, and Lincoln, and King's Lynn, and Hertford—wherever he went, he sent me a post-card of it, and a letter.

Then just about a month before the baby was due he was supposed to be coming to see me on a visit, and he didn't turn up. No letter from him, nothing. Day after day I kept expecting to hear and I didn't, just silence there was, I couldn't think what had happened, but I knew something must be wrong.

And then they come for me in my cell one day and they said 'Police visit for you, Richards, come on,' and they took me down to one of the offices in the prison. I thought it was another charge. There was two plain-clothes men there, and one of them said 'Do you know a man called Jack White?'

'Look' I said, 'it's no use asking me anything, I haven't heard from him for weeks, I don't know anything about him, I've been in here for four months and I don't know where he is, and I wouldn't tell you anyway if I did.'

'We're not looking for him' he said, 'We know where he is. He's murdered. His wife's stabbed him to death.'

They wanted a statement, but I couldn't think of anything else to say but 'I knew Jack White. We were going to be married but we're not now.' Then they went away and left me alone.

When my baby was born soon after, they took it off me in the prison hospital and sent it out into care, they thought I was going to turn against it, I suppose. I saved up all the sleeping pills they gave me, and then I took them all at once. It was lovely, it was like being in the dead house, I was asleep for two days. Then I got hysterical and I started fighting and saying why didn't they let me die. They came with this heavy jacket thing that they put on you that fastens your arms up, and they put me in a cell without any furniture in, called a strip-cell.

They let me out of there after a bit and tried to get me to go to work in the tailor's or the jam factory. Sometimes I did, so I could start a fight with somebody, and when I did that I got put down on the punishment cells where I was left like I wanted to be, all on my own.

One of the girls showed me a bit in the paper one day about Jack's wife. She'd got clean away with it, she was discharged; she'd said in court it was accidental, they'd had a fight and the knife got stuck into him by mistake. So that was the end of it, for her.

I spent a lot of time in the hospital in Holloway, I used to sit by the window and look out, and when anybody came I told them to go away and leave me alone. The doctor came in one day, and he said 'Oh Little tuppence' he said, 'Little tuppence—what's the matter with you?' I didn't answer him anything, I suppose he thought he could make me laugh.

Jack, you see, he was the only feller really who ... he was so good to me, he didn't want no trouble ever ... he was so kind to me, so good, he just wanted to settle down with me, I know he did. If we could have done that instead of me getting the three years, I don't think I'd ever have went back to prison again, not ever ... and he would never have been dead to-day. He was so good to me, Tony. It was really ... it was really my fault, you see, wasn't it, he died ...

Click-clicking, the lighter was going, its flame flicking off and on steadily, her eyes staring at nothing, and small tears running after one another down her face.

* * * * * * *

Some nights were better than others; some nights she made a cup of tea or coffee, and chattered perched cross-legged in her chair like a decorative puppet on a miniature stage.

Yes, to-day I feel better, I've been brighter the last few days, I've been to the doctor's and he's given me some pills; they've seemed to calm me down somehow, make me worry less about things. I've had a letter from Peggy, she was the girl in the next cell to me. Oh, she cried and cried when I went out, we'd got real fond of each other, you know? She's got another year to do yet, she didn't want me to go out. No, I can't write to her, and she can't write to me either: we're both convicted, you see, so they don't let us write.

Well, this is what they call a 'stiff', an illegal letter, it doesn't come out through the usual channels; it's brought out by one of the girls on a working party, or by one of the officers. Would you like to read it, it's only a lot of sentimental old rubbish, but it shows my friends haven't forgot me, doesn't it?

(It was written on pages of lined paper torn from an exercise book. 'My darling, darling Diane . . .' it began, and went on in a long affirmation of affection and lasting love. In the margins round the edges were scrawled brief messages from others like inscriptions on a greetings-card: 'Good luck, Diane dear, from Sheila.' 'All my love to you, Diane: your Audrey.' 'All the best, dear. Keep your chin up. J.J.S.' The last was a prison officer, she said.)

Oh I wonder what they're all doing in there, I do miss them. My friend Margaret who's out now, I met her the other day when I was down at the shops, she told me there were all sorts of changes: all the long-termers are being sent up to Styal, D Wing is closed down, on DX Wing there's association all day—she says you wouldn't know the place at all. It's a shame really that things have got to change, isn't it?

You think always about the past, never about the future? Where you'll be six months from now, for instance?

I hope it's not back in the nick, touch wood.

You think it might be?

Oh don't wish that on me love, will you? I say three Hail Mary's every morning to Our Lady that nothing happens today, that I don't do anything I shouldn't, that I don't see a Post Office book laying around somewhere and take it and get caught for it. It's a terrible way to live, isn't it, afraid of the badness you might do?

But you don't have to do it, do you?

No, it's not that; you don't think, you see, you don't think you're going to get caught, because it's bad luck to think like that. You have to go and do it just as though you're doing a job of work; and if it comes off, well you're all right. If I got a Post Office book with a hundred quid or so in it, I'd be set up, wouldn't I?

Set up for what?

Well for a nice long holiday or something. I'd go home, back to Ireland for a bit, see my aunties, let them see how well I was doing. Then I'd come back here, get a little flat somewhere, settle down.

What would you live on?

I don't know, that's the difficulty. I'd have to get a man to live with me, I suppose—some thief or other. Being like I am, very small, men—they always seem to think I want looking after and protecting, I don't know why. It's never very difficult to get one to look after me. There's a feller in this house now—lives on the floor below, he's a thief and a gambler up the West End. He'd have me any time I'd let him.

It'd have to be somebody like him, somebody who'd move in and 'protect' me. Either that or going on the game. But that's something I've never fancied much, I don't know why. I've had friends who did it, like the girl in Bradford I was telling you about, Sandra, the one I got picked up with. I mean there it is, isn't it, on my record—convicted for soliciting—so I've already got a conviction for it before I've done it.

I suppose it's like anything else, you'd be nervous at first but after a bit you'd get used to it. I used to think in prison, Well when I come out I'll have nothing, so the quickest way to get a bit of money is to go on the bash for it. I think all that holds me back is the feeling that once you start on that game, it's very hard to give up and go back to working for ten, twelve quid a week. You don't have to get up in the morning at eight o'clock, you make your own working hours, you can go out at ten or twelve or three, you get money every day instead of once a week. There's a lot to be said for it, once you've got used to it, I suppose . . .

But I expect it'll more likely just be one bloke looking after me, like I said . . . probably someone I've not met yet, someone in the nick right now, dreaming about coming out and settling down with a nice bird—that's all they ever do dream about, isn't it?

Then I suppose I'll have another kid, I usually do. I never use birth control, you see, it's such a messy business, I think; and anyway I always leave that side of it to the man, I don't think men like women messing about with themselves. It's all in the mind anyway, isn't it—I mean, if you say to yourself you won't fall, you don't, you know what I mean? Usually it works, anyway.

It hasn't always worked for you.

No, there's my three kids, I mean four—one in Ireland, one with my friends in Bradford, two in care now. I've been unlucky with them, really, no one to stand by them. Patricia, she was lovely, she was like a great big doll, it was really like playing with a doll to take care of her, she was no trouble. When I was in Holloway last time, after I'd had the baby that was Jack's—he was a boy, I called him Stephen, oh he was lovely—the Welfare People came and they said some people wanted to adopt him and my Patricia who'd been taken into care in Yorkshire. But I wouldn't let them, I said No, they were too good for other people to have, I wasn't going to sign them away, one day I might be in a position where I could have them myself.

The prison officers kept saying 'They're too nice for you to have, Diane, you don't deserve them', they got me really wild about it, so I made up my mind no one else was going to have them ever, but me. I suppose it's selfish really, but I've got this hope one day to have them, if I meet a man who's prepared to take them on.

What sort of a man would he be?

Well, if you want me to be really honest, no sort of man at all. I'd just like the kids and to be left on my own. I know that's not possible: like I've told you, I'll have to get one to look after me. But I honestly don't fancy the idea. I might have done with Jack, if he'd stayed alive, perhaps we might have got married and settled down. But now he's gone, it's beside the point—and if I could be, I'd sooner be on my own.

You see—I suppose I'm funny really, but I've never —well, I've never enjoyed sex with a man. I just seem like ice, I don't seem able to get into the mood at all unless I have a good bit to drink first, and then I'm not worried one way or the other. But I don't really enjoy it, ever. I know it means a lot to men, and as far as I'm concerned, if that's what keeps them happy, well alright. But it's more to oblige, it's just one of the things that goes with living with a man. Poaching an egg for him, washing his socks, letting him play about with you in bed—they're all the same to me, I don't mind particularly which.

What do you want out of life most of all?

Oh most of all I'd like a little house of my own, a bit of furniture and my children. I don't want the world, just to be reasonably happy, that's all. Like all these normal people you see, people who have their own house and go out with their children, they all seem to be reasonably happy enough. I think I'd like to be like them.

Are these straight people that you want to be like?

No, not really, it's only a very vague idea. I'm not straight and I never shall be.

All the people who live here in this house are criminals: I got this room through one of them, someone who knew one of the girls I was inside with. These are all I've got, these people, the only friends I've got in the world.

They're good people, in their own way. If they know it's your turn and you've only just come out of the nick, they'll see you all right, they won't let you starve or have nowhere to live. They'll say 'Go on, cop this,' and give you a couple of quid or so, or they'll say 'Come round to my place, you can stay there for a bit.' The men, well they want something in return for it, but I don't mind, why not, they've been good to me so I'll be good to them. Some bloke, he might be going out on a job that night and he might be going to get nicked for it and put inside for a year or two: well at least his last night he was happy, he was enjoying himself, wasn't he?

The after-care authorities—you wouldn't go to them for help when you came out?

Not unless I had to—only to report to them, when I was on licence. They'd put you in a hostel to stay when you came out if you left it to them, but I don't want that, I don't need it, I'd sooner be with my friends. The After-Care'll give you a pound now and again, and a bit of a talking to, but that's all. If I was in trouble, I'd keep right away from them. Your licence after a sentence of Corrective Training says you must lead an honest sober and industrious life, and mustn't mix with people of bad character. That's a laugh—I don't know any other kind: and anyway, I'm 'of bad character' myself, so I suppose I mustn't mix with myself.

Once you're over this side of the fence, you know, you stay on it. Well, look, love—I don't even know *anyone* who's straight, apart from you.

* * * * * * *

Some nights were worse than others; she would sit awkwardly upright in a kitchen-chair in the middle of the room, her hair uncombed, her face white. She would bite her nails, smoke one cigarette after another, wander round the room, stopping sometimes to look uneasily at herself in the mirror, or stare out of the window over the rows of roof-tops blackening in the coming night . . .

I dreaded you coming tonight, I did. This is the only time when I really start looking at myself, thinking about myself, I get a kind of choking feeling, the front that I put up comes down and I'm right at my worst.

I can't offer you a cup of tea tonight even, I'm sorry, I haven't got a thing, not a scrap of tea or a drop of milk or anything. I haven't been to work all this week or last, I just can't get up the energy to do anything, go anywhere, talk to anyone. My luck'll have to change, won't it? I can't go on feeling like this, it'll either have to get better or it'll have to get worse. How I'm feeling now, right this minute, is I could just lie on the floor there and cry me eyes out. I wish, I really do wish I was back in prison, and if I can't go back in prison I wish I was dead.

Everything's against me this time when I've come out, it's been terrible, it really has this time. Going on living, feeling frightened of what you might do, of the badness inside you coming out, and getting picked up and going back inside again . . . You want to go back and yet you're terrified you'll do something that'll get you sent back. It's a crazy way to live. Well, live—you can't call it that, it's just existing, that's all, existing without any point in it, not knowing why, not thinking about what might be coming tomorrow because it might be even worse. What's happiness for a person like me?

Last Friday I had five pounds eighteen shillings from the N.A.B. That left me two pounds eighteen after I paid the rent; I bought some food, paid some 'bus fares when I went to Highbury to see some friends, and I gave Bill ten bob last night because he wanted some fags, and that's it. Oh, and I had a few more bob, too, that I got back out of the telly there, with a knife fiddling about at the back of the slot-container. I cracked it; when they come round to collect the money they'll know someone's been at it. I'll say it wasn't me, I'll say it was like that when they brought it, they can't prove it wasn't, can they? They wouldn't do much, anyway, would they, there was only eight bob in it?

I was packing tonight, before you came; I was packing and I was going to go. Then I thought I'll wait for you. There's me case, see, put on the chair all ready with the letters in it.

They're Jack's letters, they're the first things I pack when I feel like this. I put them in the case ready for off, it makes me feel I've started packing and I'll soon be ready to go. His letters and his post-cards. I told you about those, didn't I—how he used to send me one from wherever he was working? I'll show you them. This one's from Cambridge; this is a picture of King's Lynn; this is Hunstanton—where's that, it's a holiday place, isn't it? Ely, March. These were when he was up in Yorkshire, look—Scarborough, Whitby, Hull 'Oh. my Darling'—he just used to write things like that, see, that's all, on the back. His letters . . . this was one he wrote me after I'd told him I was going to have the baby. It's in pencil, I don't know if you can still read it, it's so worn. 'You have made me so happy darling to think we are going to have a baby together that is ours. I know it is going to be a boy. I hope the poor little mite isn't going to look like his dad though, that would be hard luck for him, wouldn't it? I love you with all my heart my darling, I really do . . .'

So you see, that's it, that's all you've got left, memories and a few bits of paper. You'd never have thought to look at him Jack could ever write letters like that, you wouldn't, honest; he was so quiet and didn't have much to say for himself, you know.

Perhaps after you've gone I'll unpack them again, take them out, put them back in the drawer. It just sweeps over me sometimes, I suddenly think I'll pack up and go, and go down to the railway station, and if I talk nice to the station-master he'll give me a chance, he'll let me have a ticket.

Where to? Well back there, of course, back to Manchester, to find out where Jack's buried, so I can go and see what they've done to him, where they've put him, where he is.

It makes my arm burn to talk like this, it always does when I think like this about him. It burns here, you know, under the sticking-plaster on my fore-arm, it itches and itches until I have to tear it off. I've had it off three times already today and then put it back. I'm not going to look at it again. You can look at it. Pull it off and tell me if it's still there . . . Yes, that's right, just his name tattooed with a needle and boot-blacking. He said it was so everyone would know I was his. Now he's dead sometimes it seems to be looking at me, I'm terrified of it. I can feel the needle and his fingers when he was doing it. Cover it up again for me . . . It drives me mad, itching.

* * * * * * *

Through the long hot summer evenings, tiny, appealing and feminine, she talked softly and haltingly, her Irish voice in ironic counterpoint to over-dramatic musically-impregnated dialogue bellowing from the endless serials on the television sets in adjoining rooms.

Sometimes for short periods she was working; in a bakery once, and another time as a shop-assistant in the local branch of a well-known grocery-chain. But frequently she was 'off sick', staying in her room for days at a time, making effort neither to see a doctor nor to communicate with the people she was supposed to be working for. After a while she would decide it was no use trying to go back anyway, because by then her job would have been taken by someone else. Having no insurance stamps on her card while she was in prison she was not eligible for sickness benefit. When she went to the National Assistance Board, which she did occasionally, the Visiting Officer who came to see her was generous, both in speeding-up payment, and in personal invitations to her to go and see him at his home: he left his address and telephone number. ('Men' she had said—'They always seem to think I want looking after and protecting, I don't know why . . .')

Every feller I meet, I keep measuring them up against Jack, none of them ever seem like he was, none of them ever will, I know, because it's me, not them, that there's something wrong with. You just keep wondering and wondering and thinking and wondering what you're going to do, and you can't see any end to it at all.

Seven pounds ten a week I'm earning when I'm working: three pounds out of that for me rent, a pound for fares, a pound they take off me for tax ... it doesn't seem worth it, I'm not getting anywhere, I never will.

Yesterday the manager went out for his lunch, he left his keys on the desk in his office—the shop key, the safe key, everything. We sell candles in the shop, I could easy have taken an impression of them and given them to Bill downstairs, him and his mates'd have been in and cleaned the place out, we could all have gone to Blackpool for a fortnight on the proceeds. But I didn't, though I don't know why. At the moment I just can't seem to get enthusiastic for anything, not even thieving.

You know, you asked me one night a bit ago where I thought I'd end up, I was thinking about it after you'd gone. I thought 'Yes that's right, well where shall I end up then?' And I thought 'Well there's only two places I could end up really, during the next year or two—either back in prison, or religious-mad in a convent.'

I can't see any other prospect. Who would want me now but those places, or a man who was a thief himself, who'd have me for a bit for his bird? My own family, me aunties and that, they don't want to know me any more: when I go to prison they just write once to say how shocked they are, and then no more, except at Christmas to say they hope I'm going to church.

Because what I am, Tony, really, is just an ordinary criminal, that's all, someone who tries to live by my wits and doesn't care about things, just goes on in the same old happy-go-lucky way. Only not happy with it, and not lucky either.

I don't care for nobody really, and I don't really think anybody's ever really cared for me since my mother. It hurts for me to say that, but all the same I think it's true.

I look at myself, I try to look at myself and see myself as you see me, and I say 'What does he see when he looks at me? Well it can only be one thing, can't it, Diane' I say to myself, 'because here you are, and this is how he must see you—young, Irish and bloody useless, in a bare bed-sitter in Balham. Aren't I right?'

JOE BISHOP

BURGLARY

AGE: *30*
NUMBER OF CONVICTIONS: 7
TOTAL TIME SPENT IN PRISON: *4 years 6 months*

III

Joe Bishop

SHE lived nowhere, for she had nowhere to live; she belonged nowhere, because there was nowhere she could gain acceptance.

Perpetual outcast, she existed in a constant and unchanging pattern of constantly-changing places: institution, prison, hospital, hostel, back-street room, dosshouse. Often when she had nowhere to go she walked round streets all night, or slept in shop doorways, in 'bus shelters, in station waiting-rooms, on benches, or in derelict buildings in holes in the ground. 'If you wanted to' she said, 'you could put down my whole life under just one heading: Eviction.'

Fifteen minutes, forty minutes, once even an hour late the figure would appear, coming slowly along the street: duffle-bag over shoulder, head down, feet splayed out. A round fleshy face, big nose, thin lips, grey eyes always avoiding the direct glance, short cropped hair chopped in a ragged black fringe on the forehead. Short nail-bitten nicotined fingers cupping a cigarette, long arms dangling out of the sleeves of a rough navy-serge leather-on-the-shoulders workman's jacket; bulky body top-heavy over thick legs in tight concertina-wrinkled jeans; heavy black crepe-soled lace-up shoes . . . At a glance, a rather aggressive-looking young labourer in his early twenties, perhaps.

* * * * * * *

I do get to thinking sometimes I ought to make a bit more effort about the way I look, really. You know, not go quite so far with it as I do. I start thinking I ought to, well, at least wear women's slacks instead of men's trousers like these with zip flies, and women's casual shoes instead of real heavy men's. I mean it's to my own advantage, isn't it? Otherwise women who might like the idea of going with another woman, they can't even tell that you *are* a woman, so they're not interested because they think you're a man.

Mind you, I only think about it: I never get round to doing anything. For one reason, I've never got the money to buy a new set of clothes, and I don't suppose I ever shall. If I had that much money, it wouldn't go on clothes, that's one thing certain. So you see it's hopeless, I can never make the effort to tone it down, not one little bit. There's a lot of the girls don't like it you know; they don't mind you wearing drag in private, but they don't think you ought to be as butch as I am, not in public anyway.

People look at you in the street, you can tell what they're thinking, Is that a man or a woman? To me there's no such thing as a division like that: I'm just a person, I've never known what it's like to be any different, to me it's just ordinary, it's me, it's not anything extraordinary. It's not only that I don't like men, I've never met one in my life that I liked, not even to knock about with: my friends have always been girls. I never even knew what it was all about until I was about eighteen or nineteen and got into prison. Up till then I'd been doing things without realising, without thinking I suppose; it never crossed my mind there was anything unusual about it.

Sometimes people say 'Well haven't you ever wanted to be normal?', questions like that. But you see, to me I *am* normal, I don't even know what they're talking about. I just know I can't be anything different, there's nothing even to think about concerning it. I don't want to change, the whole idea seems plain ridiculous.

They tried to change me in mental hospital once, put me on what they called a Rehabilitation Unit because I had no fixed abode and was wandering about and was on the drugs. Five months I stayed there, and then I left—unrehabilitated. I went on that group-therapy caper, you all sit and talk about one another. I just listened and kept my mouth shut, even when they were talking about me. I got really bored stiff with it, didn't join in once. I was just eyeing the field—you know, thinking Well *you* look as though you might be game for a bit of a tickle, and I rather fancy *you*; you I'm not so keen on, you'll be ready and willing, you won't, you will, you will . . . They slung me out of it after a bit.

That was a few years back now. I've kept myself to myself pretty much since then, at least as far as talking's concerned. Who wants to know someone like me, anyway? And when they do get to know me, they're not all that keen on keeping up the acquaintance.

I'm thirty now, so that'd mean I was born 1935 sometime, I think it was in September. I'm not sure where, I expect it was somewhere in London. The first thing I remember is being in a big children's hospital, lying on my back, watching the other children over the other side of the ward all running about. I can remember my legs all in plaster, and walking about on crutches, but

I couldn't tell you what was wrong with me. When you're a child you don't know what's happening, do you? I've got an idea I'd fallen out of a window or something like that or maybe it was rickets or a TB spine or something: I know I was in altogether for something like three or four years.

I remember them trying once to get me to walk along a white line painted on the floor. Another time I was standing up in my cot out on a verandah, and pulling big pieces of dead skin off my legs, and a nurse came rushing up and ticked me off about it.

No, I don't ever remember anybody coming to see me at all. But I do recollect the war being on, and the bombing, and lying there one night crying and looking at the wall because I'd got the idea it was going to be bombed down and all big black beetles were going to come crawling out. Daft ideas kids get, don't they?

Oh yes, that's funny—now I've started talking about it I remember something else that I'd forgotten all together . . . a birthday card—or was it a Christmas card? Anyway, I remember being thrilled to bits getting it. It was on my locker at the side of the bed, and it had a picture of some flowers on it. Yes, that's it, it had a 6 on it, so it must have been a birthday card, musn't it?

Who was it from?

I don't know. It'd be from my mother, I expect, wouldn't it? Or it might not, no, it might have been from one of the nurses perhaps. It wasn't because it was from a particular person I was pleased, it was just that I was thrilled at getting it, you see.

I do remember my mother coming for me when I came out of the hospital, and I can remember holding her hand and walking very carefully over a whole pile of bricks and rubble and that, in the street where we were going. It was dark, it must have been at night, or perhaps late in the afternoon in winter.

When we got to the place she was living in, I think it was Finsbury Park somewhere, there was this big bare room with a wooden floor and not much furniture in it, and three other kids there, all babies, well one a baby and the others a bit older, but all of them younger than me. They were my brother and sisters, she said.

We all lived in this room together. My father was in the army, and my mother went out to work down the street somewhere, at a factory I think, and came in at dinner-time to give us our dinner. She was quite nice but not very affectionate with me because the others had come along: I'd only been the youngest one once, and I wasn't at home then.

I can remember my father coming home on leave a few times, but he and my mother used to go out to the pub and drink a lot and come back rowing at each other. After a bit I think I was evacuated: anyway, I know I went somewhere else to stay with another woman, out in the country somewhere, I think it might have been Wales. My father came to see me once; he brought me some sweets and gave me a flying angel, you know, twirling me round and round. My mother didn't come to see me, I think she'd gone somewhere else with the others.

Then where did I go? Oh yes, I was moved into a sort of children's home after that. Perhaps I'd become too much for the woman who was supposed to have me, I can't tell now.

Thinking back about it, I don't seem to have been much at home ever. It always seemed like a place I'd just got back to from somewhere. I think I must have been to a couple of other places that I don't even recall now, because sometimes things suggest places to me that I can't even remember being in at all. You know those baby rusks, like brown toast they are? I had one of those to eat a few years back and it suddenly gave me the idea I'd eaten one before, sitting at a table with oilcloth on it with a lot of other kids and eating those things. It even brought back the smell of the oilcloth.

And then that sort of tied up, or seemed to, with something I'd never been able to understand properly —about remembering coming home once, and all the kids from down the street were shouting things at me when they saw me about 'loony bins', and screwing their fingers round and round against their heads. So I've got the idea now that perhaps once I was in some sort of mental place for children, and that was where I ate the rusks.

I went to all sorts of different schools, but never to any one for long enough to be able to remember much about it. One day, I must have been about 11 or 12 I should think, me and my brother and sisters all decided we didn't like our mother any more, and we were going to go and live on our own. Another girl from down the street said she was coming too. She brought a couple of pans from her home, and we took some money that'd been given us to do the shopping with, and we went on the Tube right out as far as we could to the end of the line, beyond Ealing somewhere I think it was.

Then we set off walking and we ended up in some woods. By then we all felt hungry so we pinched a cabbage off an allotment we passed, and chopped it up with a dirty old spade. We put it in one of the pans with some water, and tried to cook it over a fire we made with wood and paper. It never got any hotter than just warm. We started to eat this, and my brother burst out crying: I remember getting really annoyed with him, and saying 'You're not supposed to have any dinner when you run away, don't you know that?' We found a tree with some nuts on it, and we bashed open the shells and ate those. Then when it began getting dark I said I wanted a cup of tea and I was packing up and going back home. When we got there I was scared, I sent my brother in, I wouldn't go in myself. He came out and said 'Mum says if you come in straight away, she won't hit you.' So I went in. She was standing behind the door waiting for me with a broom-stick in her hand; she really belted me with it.

We never saw any more of my father. I don't know what happened to him, he went off somewhere. We all went on living with mother, and I think she had another kid as well, I know there were four or five of us. We were always very short of money. One time she took us to Barkers I think it was, in Kensington, or perhaps it was Pontings, and went round picking things up, hats and gloves and scarves, and telling us to hide them under our clothes.

I used to go into Woolworth's myself near where we lived, pinching toys and books and sweets. I went in one Christmas time and took about ten or twelve different things I liked, and then went home and put them all in a cupboard. On Christmas morning I took them out and gave them to myself. I pretended to get really excited over them, as if they were presents I'd just been given and never seen before. There was one of those balloons you blow up in the shape of a clown, with cardboard feet so you couldn't knock it over, a toy sweet-shop, a big plastic car, some picture books and I don't know what else, I really had a terrific Christmas that time.

Did you take anything for your brothers and sisters?

No, I got them just for me. They could do their own knocking off if they wanted Christmas presents.

I think it was not long after that we got evicted into the street, and all of us had to go into different children's homes. I was the oldest, 13, and I went to a Barnado's place for girls, somewhere in Hertfordshire I think it was.

My mother came to see me once. I was very surprised about it when I heard she was coming. What she'd come for was to tell me she couldn't come again, because all the children were scattered around in different places and she couldn't afford the fares to go round seeing us all. So as I was the eldest she knew I wouldn't mind if she missed me out.

That was a sort of refrain to my childhood, I think, about being the eldest and not minding about things. I do think sometimes it could have been some of the others who got missed out now and again.

I was at Barnado's for nearly three years; I was a real lone wolf there, used to go long walks on my own, and sit reading books by myself. The other girls were always hanging round in the drive talking to the local boys. Sometimes they were allowed to bring them in the sitting-room. All I ever said to the visitors was 'Give us a couple of fags will you?' and then when I'd got them I'd walk off.

I had my first real friend at Barnado's. She was a girl a bit older than me, we used to get into each other's beds in the dormitory after the lights had gone out. When she left I tried to get some of the other girls going, to replace her, but I got moved myself soon after that out to a working girls' hostel, and was sent to work in a canteen at a local factory, washing-up and working on the counter. There was a woman there, about forty I think she was, very small and dark, and I got really friendly with her and keen on her. One day when she wasn't there I asked where she'd gone and someone told me she was away on her honeymoon, she'd got married.

I thought 'Well I'm going to kill her, nobody else is going to have her'; so when I got my wages I went into a sports shop and I bought one of those air pistols—the big heavy ones. I kept it in the hostel until the day she was due to come back to work. then I took it in with me and hid it in my locker under a tea-towel. It was just my luck, that very same day at work they had a search for some things which were missing, tins of salmon I think it was, and they found the gun in my locker and reported it back to the hostel.

They put me in a remand home and had me sent for a psychiatric report; I don't know what it said, but I wasn't charged with anything, just sent to another working-girls' hostel and given another job at a different factory. I think I was bound over never to see the woman again, something like that. I used to walk up and down the road where I thought she lived, all the same, for hours on end. But I never did see her again.

The new hostel was stricter than the old one. They had all sorts of rules about what time you were to be in at night and so on; and I was always getting into trouble there. I used to take bottles of V.P. Wine in to the dormitory, and get the girls going on it, and pornographic books and things; so eventually I got slung out. I'd nowhere to go and I was wandering round the streets when a policeman stopped me and asked me where I lived. I said I'd nowhere, so he told me to go to an L.C.C. dosshouse in Dovehouse Street. You get a mattress on the floor and one blanket to put over you, and you pay a couple of bob for it, or do a bit of work in the morning, chopping wood or cleaning. You can only stay three nights, then you have to move on.

Obviously, I thought, I'd have to do something, I

couldn't just drift. I was nearly 17 by then, so I joined the women's Army, and was sent to a training camp near Aldershot. Not long after I got there I started having an affair with one of the corporals who was training us. We were writing passionate love letters to each other and leaving them in each other's bunks, and one of mine to her got found. She was reduced to the ranks, and I was told they didn't think I was suitable for the Army, so I didn't even complete the initial three months' training which they use to sort out the weeds from the flowers. Straight off, they had me out as one of the weeds.

After that I had another factory job, with the Dunlop rubber people; they found lodgings for me too. Then I had a row with the landlady: she objected because I came back very late one night, and when she didn't come and open the door I smashed the glass and broke in. She chucked me out the next day. I took my case down to the left luggage at Victoria, and went up the West End, Wardour Street and Berwick Street, wandering round there, looking at the clubs I'd heard about.

There was one coffee bar I went in, I was just sitting there drinking, and I noticed girls kept coming in and going downstairs one after another, so I thought I'd see what was going on. I went to the top of the stairs and the man at a counter behind the espresso machine called out at me 'It's ladies only down there, mate.' I just gave him a cold look and said 'Well what do you think I am, then?' He sort of looks at me hard for a minute, and then he says 'Oh': so down I went.

That's a thing I get quite a lot of, you know, in toilets and that sort of place. At first the attendant very often tries to stop me going in until I tell them. Or a landlady'll say, if I go about a room, 'I'm sorry, it's for females only.' Mind you, some can tell straight off without having to be told: the more intelligent ones.

Anyway I went downstairs at this coffee bar, and underneath is a big room with a juke box and subdued lighting and little tables and chairs. And it's all women, dancing with each other, necking with each other, and nobody bothering about it, it was fabulous. I stayed there all night, it seemed the most marvellous place in the world. The girls were all taking pills and smoking reefers, and some of them were 'popping', it was terrific. After a bit one of them came up to me and she said 'What's your name, then?' I said 'Joe Bishop,' and she said 'Hello Joe, nice to meet you.'

Why 'Joe'?

I don't know, I just fancied it. My name's really 'Jean', so at least it begins with the same letter, doesn't it? But 'Hello Joe'—that sounds really nice, I think. When she said it like that the first time, it was just as though I was being christened or baptised, it felt absolutely right. I've never used any other name since, I even make them put it on my record in prison. 'That's my name' I say, and they can't do anything about it.

I had a kind of coming home feeling in the club, as though I'd reached somewhere I belonged for the very first time. I went in every night, and stayed there most of the day too, just talking and snoozing and listening to the music until my money ran out, which was about four days. Then I got up and said to some of the girls 'I won't be long,' and they all said 'O.K. Joe, be seeing you,' and I went out in the street. There was only one thing I needed, and that was a bit of money; and then I could go straight back in the club again.

I walked down the street, it was afternoon I remember, wandered around for a bit looking for somewhere to get what I wanted, and then ahead of me I saw a doorway, like the entrance to a flat, between two shops. It was open so I dodged in; there were some stairs going up to a little entrance hall. I crept up those, and gave one of the doors at the top a little push, and it opened into a small sort of office, with a desk and a lot of papers and files and things. I called out to see if there was anyone about: there wasn't a sound.

There didn't look to be anything worth having, but I thought I'd go through the desk drawers just to see. In the second one down there was one of those metal petty-cash boxes: it wasn't locked and I opened the lid, there was about fifteen bob in silver in it. I scooped that up, put it in my pocket, and ran out; down the stairs, round the streets, back to the coffee bar, and straight down into the club again. I don't think I can have been gone more than about a quarter of an hour altogether. There it was, I was back again with enough money to go on for another day or two. I felt really pleased with myself about it.

A few days later of course I had to go out again. This time I wasn't so lucky, no open doors to offices. But I got round the back of some car showrooms, found an open window, wriggled in, and had a prowl around several passages and stairways until I found a shilling-in-the-slot electric meter. I gave it a few clouts with a piece of brick I found, and got it open; it was worth about two quid altogether in shillings.

I went on like that, regular, for quite a time. But it was all small stuff, a few bob here and a few bob there, mostly out of meters and drawers. What I was thinking about I don't know—I was very green in those days— but I kept a little notebook and I wrote down 'Jobs Done' in it: a list of all the places I'd been in and how much money I'd got. '36 Love Street, meter, 17/-.

Dawes Place, offices, 35/-.' All set out like that, absolutely stupid, it was.

I'd had too much to drink in Great Windmill Street one night and I was picked up by the Law. Of course when they searched me, there it all was, written down for them, in this notebook. I don't think they could believe it at first, until they started checking-up with the different addresses and found they all matched.

Nine months I got for it from the magistrates, and I was taken straight off to Holloway. Right to the top in one go, you might say—prison first time, with no little approved schools or borstals or anything like that to begin with.

Quite frankly, I was a bit excited about the prospect of prison. Only the week before I'd been up to Holloway with two other girls, visiting one of the club girls we knew who was inside. And now there I was, going in myself. I was on the same wing as her when I got in there, so it didn't seem all that lonely; and it wasn't strange or frightening, because it was exactly like all the girls had said it was.

When I came out I was supposed to be on licence, but I didn't bother to report to the After-Care, I went straight back to the club. Three or four days later two policemen came in and pulled me out, and I went back to prison for not keeping to the terms of the licence, not working and leading an 'undesirable' life. When I came out again of course I was no longer on licence and they couldn't touch me, and I was back in the club the same day. Only it wasn't the same one, it was under another name and in another place, because the police were always closing the West End clubs down, or trying to.

One way and another I went on for a few years leading that sort of life, with the difference that I got steadily more and more hooked on the drugs. First it was Benzedrine—you know, the cotton wool out of those inhaler things, it could give you a lift for an hour or two if you rolled it up and swallowed it. Then it was weed, marijuana; and finally it was heroin, injecting with a needle—what they call 'popping'.

Marijuana you smoke: you either sprinkle it on some tobacco and roll it up in a cigarette, or you have a whole roll-up of it. If you do it too much you can get the horrors, persecution-mania, you know, you think everyone's watching you from doorways and staircases, things like that. If you smoke too little, it just gives you fits of giggles.

But if you've got it nicely balanced, the amount you're taking I mean, it's very nice, everything's amusing but you're detached from it. You take the smoke right deep down into your lungs, and keep it there as long as you can, trying not to let it out. Music always sounds marvellous and dreamy, all the people you're with seem really friendly and nice, and you get an all-over warm sexiness that's great, it doesn't make you shy any more, you can just enjoy it with the other girls, all of you together.

I wrote a poem once when I was on it, well not exactly a poem but a piece of prose that I wrote out with short lines and that, like poetry. It looked really good when it was done out like that. I can still remember it, yes. I gave it a title, I called it 'The Photograph'....

> I carried her into the bedroom
> Where I laid her tenderly down.
> She smiled up at me
> But said nothing.
> I stroked her cheek with my finger.
> She still smiled
> But remained cold and unresponsive.

> I whispered to her
> But only the echo of my voice
> Returned
> I realised I was alone with only
> Her photograph.

Everybody thought it was terrific at the time. I still like it myself.

And the great thing about weed is that you don't become addicted. If you can't get it, it doesn't drive you potty. I've never been able to understand why the police and the courts are so down on it: if it was freely available it would give people who liked it a lot of pleasure and do no harm to anyone, or at least no more than alcohol does. I know people who never touch anything else, and I can't see they're doing any harm to anyone. If we had big firms importing it, like we have big firms distilling gin and brewing beer and offering it for general sale, of course then it wouldn't be illegal. But it no more leads you on to the other drugs that you get addicted to, than beer leads you on to horse-racing.*

Heroin of course, that's different. Then you're really fizzing when you get on that. It's a sort of combination of feelings really, high and at the same time tranquil, as though you were drifting in a canoe on a peaceful river. You're right above the world, looking down on it, everyone else is nice but unimportant, you're the big one yourself, you're a giant, physically, intellectually, every way. I got on to it through a friend—well, she wasn't a friend until we became friendly, if you know

---

* (This seems to be correct; a somewhat similar argument is advanced by Dr. Peter Hays, Senior Lecturer in Psychiatry at St. George's Hospital, London, in his *New Horizons In Psychiatry* (Penguin Books 1964), pp. 188-199. T.P.).

how I mean. She was a junkie herself, and one day she asked me if I'd like to try a fix at the same time as her so I said Yes.

Naturally the first one's free, and the next couple or three after that might be. Then when you've got right on it, really hooked, then you have to start to pay for the tablets. Of course the girl, she's paying for her own supplies so if she can get someone else on it, it helps her with her finances, and that's the way it goes, through a whole chain of people. At the beginning of the line you'll often find someone who's a registered drug addict and getting supplies on the National Health, far more than he needs for himself, and then selling the rest. A lot of the pushers I know are doing it not to make a lot of money or corrupt the young or any of that stuff, but to earn the money to buy their own. Prices vary, but it's usually about a pound for four or five tablets now.

You use one at a time, put it in a teaspoon with a few drops of water, and then warm it over a match until it's dissolved. Then you draw the liquid up in a hypodermic, and slide it in under your skin, either in your thigh or in your arm. Some people go in for main-lining—that's injecting it straight into an artery: if you do that it takes effect in about five seconds flat. You can make your own needle if you want, for just a few coppers, by using . . . well, I'll leave that.

Getting hooked more and more on the drugs like I was meant of course that I had to have more and more money. Petty-cash boxes and electric meters just weren't good enough, so I had to go out of the West End looking for jobs, out to Holland Park and places like that where the big houses are. I'd go in the evenings and walk round looking for suitable places— houses with plenty of good-quality stuff in them, and with ground-floor windows that had the sort of catches on them that could be easily opened with a screwdriver or a knife. I didn't mind whether there were people in the houses or not: I'd wait until they'd gone to bed, and then in I'd go, with my rubber soles and my little flashlamp, and I never made a sound.

I really liked breaking into people's homes, I used to have a good old look round at everything, sit down in the arm-chairs and have a little rest, just looking round the room, shining my flash-lamp around and thinking 'This is really nice this place is, it must be really good living here, it's so smart and comfortable.' There were times when I had to literally force myself to get up and start putting things in my pockets: I took anything that was lying about, small ornaments, handbags, brief cases, whatever there was. Then I used to go in the kitchen, see if there was any odd money lying about in drawers or tea-caddies or jars, and sometimes have a creep upstairs as well to see what was up there. I never thought of it as stealing, I was really enjoying myself so much; in a way it was like being on a kind of treasure-hunt.

Back down the clubs there were always plenty of people you could sell small things to. But you never got anywhere near the full value: solid gold cuff-links I've let go for thirty bob, and rings for a pound each, because I was never worried about making a lot of money, only wanting a few pounds just to keep myself going for the next day or two, and then when that was gone going out and getting some more.

But I was always getting caught. It was because I spent far too much time in the houses, I'd never go straight in and out again. One place I was still there at 9 o'clock in the morning when they were all getting up for breakfast. Another place a man punched me straight in the face and knocked me down. When he found out I was a woman he felt really sorry about it and apologised to me.

I got 6 months, a year, 2 years, oh I can't remember them all. Once I got done for waving a knife at a man when I was in a 'phone box, he wanted to get in so I came out swearing at him and threatening to cut him: he ran off for the Law and when they came back, him and two policemen, he kept shouting at me 'You Teddy Boys are going to be taught a lesson!' He was another who felt bad about it when they said in court I wasn't a boy.

Being caught so often, perhaps that was what prevented me ever really getting so far gone on the drugs that I couldn't recover. I used to feel pretty shocking for a few weeks, cold shivers and sickness and all that sort of thing. On the whole the prison doctors used to let me down easy by giving me dope to get over the initial stages.

Onetime the After-Care people made a big effort to try and get me away from the life in the clubs, they got me a job for when I came out of prison in the Channel Isles, fixed me up to work on a farm there, bought my ticket, put me on the boat, everything.

It only lasted a week, I just wasn't used to that sort of life I suppose. As soon as I got my first wages I hopped on the boat and came straight back to London, with a new shirt and a fiver to start me off back in the clubs again.

Once you get down in them it's not long usually before you wind up back in prison, because you can't go in clubs and go to work, the two don't mix, so you have to find some way of living without going to work, and there's only one way I know of to do that.

I never minded going into Holloway, after all it was a place where I had lots of friends; I always get a big welcome there when I go in, all the girls shouting out 'Hello Joe, how long have you got, where've you been all this time?' I never get a warm welcome anywhere else I go, Holloway's the only place where it ever happens. Outside nobody wants me and I don't fit in: in there I'm accepted, it's all women, which suits me fine, I can't be thrown out, I really belong . . . I quite often dream I'm back inside, I've got a sentence and I don't know how long I've got, only it feels like it's going to be a long time—and I wake up feeling happy, until it begins to dawn on me it was only a dream.

* * * * * * *

Our conversations always had to take place in backstreet cafés or borrowed offices, in motor cars or during walks up and down streets trying to find addresses of rooms advertised to let. The cafés she chose were steamy and dirty; they served tea made with sterilised milk in thick chipped cups. 'Homely' was the word she used to describe them, insisting that anywhere else would make her feel uncomfortable.

When landladies opened doors, looked her up and down and said that the vacant room had just been taken ten minutes before, she complained vehemently that it was because they had seen me standing in the background and thought she was going to be the type who brought men in. When she kept me waiting in the rain at street corners, it was always because I'd been standing in the wrong place or had made a mistake about the time.

During part of the time I knew her, she was living in a mental hospital from which she went out every day to work as a groundswoman in a nearby park. She was having no treatment at the hospital, because she refused it, although she had gone in as a voluntary patient after trying to cut her wrists. She was moved from one ward to another, creating trouble wherever she was by trying to seduce the other female patients, drinking, fighting, and coming in late. When after some months of this she one day in a temper asked to be discharged, her request was granted immediately, and within an hour she was being escorted out of the hospital grounds.

Talking to Joe, and trying to find the right questions to encourage her to describe and discuss herself, I felt often like an elephant blundering about in a cornfield. For beneath her charmless, rude and often aggressive manner could sometimes be caught brief glimpses of a shy, sensitive and endearing fieldmouse of a personality, now incapable of coming out into open spaces and daylight. Everything that happened to her all through her life had driven her further and more deeply in upon herself; taught her to put up barriers and defences and conceal herself from view behind truculent non-belonging; made her try to live as though immediate instinctual gratification was the only end that was worth pursuing. It could not be said that she had no insight into her condition. She had; what she lacked completely was the wish to do anything about it.

But whoever might feel sorry for Joe and want to try and help her, it did not sound like herself, as she talked on and on in her flat bleak voice, like the wind soughing over some desolate claypit where someone had once strangled emotion to death.

* * * * * * *

You know that Peter Pan story, the little boy who never grew up, I feel that's me sometimes. I'll be walking through a park and see some swings, if there's nobody about I can't pass them, I must go over and have a little swing on my own, and a turn on the roundabout and the see-saw. Perhaps it's because I didn't get full benefit from my childhood, I want to make it up to myself like when I stole those Christmas presents when I was a kid.

I've never grown up with anything in me from childhood, you know, no talents of any kind have developed in me. People say 'Well you must be good at something, everybody's good at something:' but I'm not. There's not one single thing I can do that I'm any good at at all. When I go after a job, something I've read in the paper maybe, I don't go with the idea of thinking It sounds just like me, I must get it: I go with the idea I wonder if they'll want to know? Then when they say they're sorry I'm not suitable, I always say to myself I know; I know I'm not suitable, you don't have to tell me.

I once did have a job that suited me, with British Railways on one of their delivery vans, as a driver's mate. You didn't have to worry what you looked like, no one could have worn a skirt for it even if they'd wanted to, you were climbing in and out of the back of the van all the time, loading and delivering parcels. I was only on it three weeks, then they found out I'd been inside and that was that: the railways won't have anyone who's been in prison.

I used to have ambitions to do a few things, a long time ago. Once it was to work among books, because I love reading: in a bookshop or a library, something like that. Last year my ambition was to get a job with the council, sweeping the roads with one of those little hand-carts. Shows how your ambitions can change, doesn't it?

When I do get a job, I know it'll not be long before I get thrown out of it for something or other; not turning up, or being rude, or trying to pinch something. It's the same with a room, sometimes I seem deliberately to try and force the landlady to give me notice, by breaking in to her meter or something like that. And people, too, friends, everybody—it's the same there as well. I will keep trying to test people all the time. Some of them pass the tests, and others don't. Those that do, I have to think-up more tests for them, on and on until they fail, like they have to, in the end. I'll push them and drive them until they can't stand me any more, and tell me they don't want to have any more to do with me.

Why?

I don't know why, unless it's because I think rejection is the only thing I can really deal with, and acceptance is something I just couldn't stand. I'm used to the rejection, you see; sometimes I feel almost triumphant about it when it happens, a bit elated, because I was right about people after all, I've proved that they don't want me.

Now and again I have a go at cutting my arms or my wrists with one of the knives I carry around with me. I always do it in a toilet, I sit down and start chopping away, then I put bits of toilet-paper over the cuts and come out again. When I walk along and feel the blood running down my arms I feel better somehow, it's like letting something out of me. It gives a terrific feeling of relief, I'm not tense any more. Usually I do it when I'm angry with someone, I suppose in a way at first I feel as though I'm attacking them; then it becomes myself. There have been times when I've done it, come out and been walking down the street and suddenly felt It's not enough, I've not done it enough; and I run down the next toilet and do it some more until I feel better.

That was how I got into the hospital, through doing that. When they threw me out I did it again, but no one paid any attention. You could almost hear their sighs of relief that I was going. I felt really annoyed about it, I'd wanted to leave feeling grateful to the hospital staff instead of angry with them. During the last two months I was there and they were all getting so fed-up with me, I kept wishing I could have fits or something so that I could feel I had a right to be there and the staff would feel so too. But it didn't work out like that. Even there they couldn't put up with me, I'd pushed them until they rejected me too. That takes a bit of doing, you know, to get a mental hospital glad to get rid of you.

* * * * *

I asked her once, when she was talking about her childhood, how long it was since she'd seen her mother . . .
—Oh, a long time. Except for once, a few months ago, funnily enough; she was just in front of me in the queue at Hammersmith Labour Exchange. She looked at me and then after a bit she said 'I know your face, don't I?'; she said 'You're Jean, aren't you?' I said 'Yes, that's right.' She said 'Yes, I thought you were, how are you?' I said 'Oh I'm all right, how are you?' She said 'Oh I'm all right thanks, yes. Hasn't it been shocking weather?'

MISS McDONALD

FRAUD

AGE: *40*
NUMBER OF CONVICTIONS: *9*
TOTAL TIME SPENT IN PRISON: *7 years 4 months*

IV

Miss McDonald

'THOROUGHLY spoilt', 'spineless', 'weak willed', 'easily led'—pejoratives like these have been used liberally and frequently, since the early days of her long history of law-breaking, in assessments of Miss McDonald's character by the judiciary and penologists.

The primary source for this aetiology of a criminal career, however, is not impersonal insight. It is Miss McDonald herself: and she had used and repeated these and several other similar phrases within the first quarter of an hour of our meeting. She has said them and heard them said about herself so often now they have become an almost spontaneous response to questioning, used to construct a self-perpetuating explanation of the inexplicable. For to Miss McDonald life has always been too difficult and complex to deal with. Some of her attempts to do so would make subjects for high comedy if their results were not so inevitably and disastrously self-destructive.

She lived with a cheerful chubby and hard-working man, whose wife deserted him some years ago, in a small neat house in an impeccable suburban road. Tall, with slender long legs, beautiful auburn hair, large brown eyes and a pale and flawless complexion, she carried herself with a willowy grace and dignity that complemented the gently undulating cadences of her quiet Lowland Scots voice. She talked happily about herself, often with animated and enthusiastic denigration, in sentences which were at times as elaborately tautologous and labyrinthine as any of Henry James'.

Perhaps it is this habit, more than any true characteristic, which has earned her the appellation 'spineless'. Certainly at many times she is unsure what course of action—if any—to commit herself to: out of a desire to please she agrees with all the good advice, however impossible of attainment, which she inspires others to give her freely. Then to their exasperation she does the opposite of what they have suggested and she has agreed with. And she feels absolutely wretched and inadequate, always, about it.

Behind stiff white lace curtains over the windows of the polished and immaculately tidy front sitting-room, beneath a flight of five china ducks going up the wall, we had afternoon tea three times a week. After it she smoked one cigarette. Then she tidied away the cups and plates, we concluded the proper observances of social enquiries about health and relatives, and conversation became less casual.

* * * * * * *

I hope you'll nae mind, Mr. Parker, switching off the tape-recording machine if Mr Hardy pops in any time for a wee chat, until he's away out of the house again? He doesna mind ma talking to you, but it's just that I havena ever said anything to him about ma being in prison and things like that, and it might upset him a bit if he haird me describing it on the tape. I always seem to be so busy looking after him, doing his washing and mending and feeding and keeping the house nice, somehow I havena found the time ever to mention it to him yet.

I tell him you've come to talk tae me about ma childhood in Scotland and that. And that's true right enough isn't it? Och though if I was a stronger person I'd have told him about it by now. I expect mebbe I will too, when I get the opportunity. But it's nae an easy thing to do tae introduce the subject, I can't seem able to lead round to it.

Well now, I promised I'd show you the photographs today, didn't I? Here they are, I got them all ready for you last night when Mr Hardy was away down the public house. This is ma mother first of all—you can see what a fine woman she is, can you not, a fine big woman? I'm not as big-boned as she is, but I take ma height from her, and my lovely complexion. But a terrible disappointment I've been to her, that's true enough what she always says. Her only child, and I've nearly broke her heart many a time, I have.

Now this here is a picture of ma grandfather; my mother's father he was. He died before I was born, but I haird ma gran and my mother talk about him often enough. You see him there in his station-master's uniform, taken outside the station just before he retired; look at his wax moustache and his cheese-cutter collar and all those gold buttons and braid on his cap! He was a fine man too. My gran used to get this picture out of her trunk and show it to me when I was young, and the gold watch he got when he retired, and some certificate or other he'd won for a brave deed once. He was a very well-known and respected person in our village, my grandfather, he was the station-master there for over twenty-five years.

Now this here is my gran, her I did know of course, because we lived with her. I was very very fond of my granny. She died when she was eighty-one, and her hair still brown, not a touch of grey in it anywhere. She used to let me take the pins out of it and brush it for her, it came right down her back to here.

She was only very small, not like the rest of the family, but she was one of the best women there's ever been, she was. She used to teach me things when I was little; she'd say to me 'If you learn now, child, it won't be so hard when you grow up.'

We had an outdoor wash-house, and she used to take me in there and show me how to use the tubs and the big wooden washing-boards. When it came to Monday washday, I always used to try and get off school by saying I was feeling poorly so I could help her with the washing, I loved doing it so much. I still do, ever since I can remember I've always loved doing the washing; I'll take other people's washing and do it for them, I just like squeezing things in the warm suds and wringing them out and making them all nice and clean and fresh.

And ironing I like, and housework, dusting and polishing and scrubbing floors, I really enjoy it. And cooking—anything to do in the house, sewing, darning, mending—whatever it is, I'm happy all day long doing it. I'm always cleaning Mr. Hardy's shoes for him, even when he says they're already clean, or pressing his shirts twice over, things like that. He says he ought to clean his own shoes at least, but I say Why, if I enjoy doing it for you?

And my granny taught me how to do embroidery as well, how to make tray cloths and dressing table sets and covers for chair backs, all things like that. She was really the best gran a child could have, she was. Another thing she told me was she was a great believer in the Co-Oper-ative; she said wherever you went in the world, you should always shop at the Co-Op, you get value for your money there. 673465 was our number, you never forget it, do you, it stays with you all your life.

I haven't any pictures of my father at all. He died when I was three, and I don't remember a thing about him. He was the porter at the railway station: my grandfather got him the job before he married my mother. And he was no good at all; my mother had a terrible life with him before he died, he drank a lot and was always gambling and things like that. She was very very unhappy with him indeed, and in a way I think it must have been a good thing when he was killed like he was, on the railway, run down one day by a train.

Of course it meant my mother had a very hard life looking after me and bringing me up on my own. That's why I had such a lot to do with my granny: she looked after me while my mother was out at work earning the money to keep us. She worked on a farm near by, and in the evenings she used to go to one of the big houses in the district where two sisters lived: they were noble people and had a lot of banquets, my mother used to help out with the catering arrangements.

All through my childhood there wasn't much money, but I had a happy life, I was very happy as a child indeed. I think in fact I was too happy. I was spoiled, my mother's always told me that she was inclined to just let me do what I liked, because I was her only child and she wanted to do too much for me.

All round where we lived in this village were beautiful woods and hills, a river and an old ruined castle. We had this little house of my grandmother's, just the two rooms downstairs and two upstairs, my gran slept in one and me and my mother in the other. My mother and I used to go out together quite a lot, to church on Sundays and then to see friends and relations. I was always very shy I remember, even when I was thirteen or so, just used to sit on the edge of the chair and not say anything, and I blushed bright red if anyone spoke to me. I was very tall and thin too, and my mother was very young-looking for her age, so everyone used to say we were just like two sisters out together.

When I was $14\frac{1}{2}$ my granny died and I left school so I could help out with the money for the family. I went to work in a Woolworth's in the nearest town. I didn't like it a lot because they didn't keep you on one counter, they moved you around. I liked the cosmetics and the jewellery, but not the electrical equipment and the household goods. After a while I got another job in a drapery store, it was much more boring but the money was better.

I didn't go out very much even then as a young girl. My mother didn't like me to, she preferred me to stay at home in the evenings and listen to the wireless with her and do embroidery together. She kept most of my wages and gave me pocket money out of it; but of course by the end of the week I'd had it all back and more, as she pointed out, because she spoiled me so much, buying very good food and keeping me comfortable and giving me everything I could want.

I moved on from the drapers when I was about 17, I think, and went to work in a factory in the town. There were a lot of girls there I got friendly with, and just sometimes I could go to a dance with them on a Saturday night. I met a Polish boy called Janeck at one of the dances and wanted to bring him home, but my mother said he wouldn't be suitable so I didn't. Then I met another boy whose father was a big man on the local council: he was called Stanley and he was 24, seven years older than me. My mother thought a lot about him, and when he asked if we could get married she said 'Yes' straight away. We got engaged, and his mother made a big fuss about it: he was her eldest boy and I think she wanted him to do better for himself. They were that sort of people, my mother said, and she told him he could come and live with us when we were married.

I became pregnant while I was engaged, when Stanley and I were in one evening and my mother had gone out. I think if you're really in love with somebody that kind of thing can happen, and I was very much in love with him. So the wedding had to be a very small affair. I'd wanted a white one, but in view of what had happened my mother said she couldn't approve of it. Instead we just had a few close relatives and friends, and I wore a plain suit, and hat and gloves. I looked very nice, I wish I had a picture to show you but I haven't got one down here in the south.

Afterwards we went on a 'bus to the seaside and we stopped at a hotel for the week-end, then my husband had to get back to his job. He worked as a site-manager for his father who was a builder. Only a few weeks after, he started saying he had to be working late at the different sites he was on. He got to coming in later and later, sometimes it was after midnight; he just didn't seem like the same person at all. One day my mother was talking to a neighbour who remarked on how often he came home late and said she'd seen him in the town one night with another woman. My mother was flabbergasted, when she came in she just sat down and couldn't speak: she wouldn't tell me what was the matter or anything, I had to beg and beg her before she'd tell me what it was. I didn't believe it when she did tell me, but my mother said she didn't think the neighbour was the type of woman to say a thing like that if it wasn't true.

We neither of us said anything to Stanley when he came in that night, but a few evenings later after he'd come in for his tea and got up and went out again my mother said 'You follow him, try and find out what he's up to.'

It was dark and I went round the back of the house and down the road to the next 'bus stop; when the 'bus came along I went downstairs on it, because I knew he'd be on the top where he could smoke. When it came into the town and stopped in the market place he got off, and I jumped off too behind him. He went straight over to the picture house, and there was a blonde lady waiting outside, and he took her arm and they went in. She looked very common, really she did.

I just felt like I was in a trance, I went back to the market place and got on the next 'bus back home. When I walked in my mother took one look at me and she said 'It's true then. Well, what did I tell you?' We sat up waiting for him until quarter to twelve when he came in, and then my mother said to him that he couldn't stay on in the house if he was going to behave like that, it would have to be one thing or the other.

He said he wouldn't do it any more, and soon after that I had the baby. When the pains started my mother went for the midwife and she came and delivered me. My mother rang up my husband at work and told him it was a boy, and he said he was going to be late home because he'd have to go and tell his parents about it on the way. He didn't seem to be interested in the child at all, and he started staying away from the house altogether because he said he had to go and work on sites that were right over on the other side of the Clyde, and I didn't see him for days at a time.

One day when the baby was about two months old I was in the house on my own, my mother was out at work and my husband was away somewhere I didn't know where. I felt I was short of money for make-up and things like that, so I took one of his suits from upstairs and went on the 'bus into the town and pawned it for £2.

He came in that same night and started looking for it to go out in. He asked me where it had gone, and what had happened to it. When I told him what I'd done, he lifted his hand and smacked my face and then he went out. He stayed away for about a week that time.

A few weeks later I'd gone into Glasgow to do some shopping one day while my mother was at home to look after the baby and let me go out, and I went into Burton's and said could I have a suit on approval for my husband, who wanted it for a special function he was going to and he couldn't get in to try it on for himself. They said yes so long as I gave them my name and address, and could show them a letter or something to prove where I lived. I did that, and they gave me the suit, and I took it straight away down a back street and sold it to a dealer who gave me £3-10-0 for it. Then I went and bought myself a jumper, and a few things for the baby.

I didn't say anything to my mother when I got back, and a week later I went back over to Glasgow and into the Burton's shop again, to tell them my husband would be coming in shortly to pay for the suit. Another week or so went by, then they sent someone to the house to enquire what was happening. I wasn't in, and my mother didn't know anything about it, so they came back again later in the evening when I was home, and asked me what I'd done with it. I told them, and my mother was in a terrible state. They said they were going to put it in the hands of the police, who came the next day. I was charged and taken to the magistrates' court. I was just 20 then.

The magistrates said I must either pay a five pound fine, or go to prison for 30 days. I couldn't pay the five pounds so that was it, I was taken to Glasgow jail for a month.

But your mother—she could have paid the fine surely, couldn't she?

I think she did try to raise the money but she couldn't; anyway she said she was sorry but she hadn't got it, and she thought it would be a lesson to me never to do anything like that again.

The magistrates didn't suggest a conditional discharge or probation—just prison right away?

Well I think perhaps they thought the fine would probably be paid. In Scotland they're generally much stricter than here, especially where women are concerned; they're very strong on women defrauding men, they don't like it at all. And of course it was a good lesson to me—I was crying all the time I was in Glasgow jail, worrying about my mother and what she'd be thinking, whether she'd have any more to do with me or not. No one else in the family had ever done a thing like this, and one of her brothers was in the police force too, oh it was terrible.

She came to see me in prison and said I'd really have to think about myself while I was in there, and make up my mind never to do anything like it again. She said my husband had been to the house and taken the baby away to live with his family; and she couldn't stop him because of course she had to go to work herself and couldn't look after it. But she said when I came out perhaps I could get the baby back again.

When I was released my mother took me to a solicitor but he couldn't do anything about the baby. I got in a very bad nervous state then, so she took me to the doctor and he said he thought I ought to go into hospital and have a course of that electrical treatment, the E.C.T. it was called. I went in as a voluntary patient in Glasgow in the September or the October, and stayed there for 8 weeks.

Twice a week they took me down to the basement and gave me this electric shock; they lie you down on a bed and put these things on each side of your head. I was very frightened of it. You feel you're falling down and down in a big pit, and when you wake up you've got a terrible headache and you feel awful. But I did feel better for it, and I came home in time for Christmas. But it was a very depressing Christmas for both my mother and me, that one was. Neither of us could enjoy it very much, we just sat and talked quietly together.

In the three months at the end of that year you—a girl of just over 20—had been in prison; in a mental hospital; lost your husband; and he'd taken your baby?

Yes. Like I say I think it got my mother down a lot, she seemed to grow much older round about that time too. After Christmas I went to work in the local brickworks, lifting bricks onto trucks. It was shift work and hard work, but at least I was earning a bit of money and trying to get myself straightened out. One night I said to my mother I think I'll go to the pictures down in the town, and in the market place there I saw my husband standing waiting for a bus on his own.

I went up and asked him could we have a talk, and we went and had a cup of tea. I asked him how the baby was and he said I wasn't to worry, the baby was fine. So then I said was there any chance of him taking me back again, and he said there wasn't at the moment, he'd have to wait and see how things went with me. When I got back I told my mother about it; she said I'd have to be very careful, I shouldn't really have anything to do with him in my position, otherwise it might create difficulties in the future.

I found the brickworks too hard really, and after a time I stopped working again and stayed at home looking after the house while mother was out. But I got very restless, and one day I went to Glasgow again, into a different men's shop, and this time I got two suits and sold them, and went on a bit of a spending spree doing shopping. I did the same thing a week later with another two suits, saying they were for my husband like before.

Of course the police came to the house again, and this time my mother was really angry about it. She said in court that whatever it was was wrong with me, I must have inherited it from my father, it wasn't from her side of the family, they were all good; but he was bad, so it must have come from him. And she said 'If she's no intentions of doing what's right herself, then there's nothing I can do for her.' This time I got six months.

She wouldn't come to see me in prison or even write to me, so I asked the chaplain what I should do and he said I ought to write her a really nice letter, and he'd put a word in for me too. I remember exactly what I wrote: 'Dear Mother' I put, 'This is to ask you if you will please forgive me for what I have done. This is really going to be the last time, and all I want is for you to forgive me. I know that what I have done is really a terrible thing, not only for myself but also for you being outside and having to meet people who know. But if you will only come to see me, I will pull myself together, I promise I will.'

The chaplain put a letter in with it like he'd promised, and about a week later she came. She was talking to the warder who was supervising the visit more than to me, telling her how they'd had nothing like it ever in her family and she couldn't understand why I did it and brought such a lot of shame on her. She said to me I'd have to leave the house, I couldn't go on living there any more.

I did feel sorry for what I'd done, and I said if she'd only give me one more chance I'd make up my mind I was going to be good. The chaplain did a lot for me, he had a talk with her about it too, and eventually my mother said she would reconsider her decision. So at the end of my sentence I was able to go back home again.

A few days after I'd got back she said she was going out to have a cup of tea with a friend, and she wanted me to go too, so over we went to this house in a village not far away. There I was introduced to the man whose house it was; he was a widower, and he had three grown-up daughters. He said to me 'You're going to be just like one of my own girls, you can come and live here and be one of us.' On the way home I said to my mother 'What does he want me to go and live there for?' and she said 'Well, he wants me to marry him, and if I do I shall be living there and selling our house of course.'

He was only a little man, much smaller than my mother, and the next week-end he and she went down into England somewhere to see his relatives. On the Monday I was at home and a telegram came, it said 'Got married today'. I shut the door and sat down, I was shocked, I felt really terrible about it, that I hadn't even been invited. To tell you the truth, it's an awful thing to say but I think I was really jealous about it and being very selfish: I wasn't thinking about my mother's future at all, and what a hard life she'd had.

The next day they came back, and then on the Wednesday a furniture van came and took away all our furniture; some of it was sold, and the rest was taken to my step-father's. I had to share a bedroom there with one of the other girls, Edith, she was the youngest one, and his favourite.

I got a job, this time in another shop, a furniture store, and I was there for quite a long time, nearly a year. Then I started getting into trouble again, taking suits from shops again and selling them; I got another six months, and then I got nine months, and then I got a year. Usually it was suits, and one time it was some blankets and bedding. My mother and my step-father were getting really ill with it, I think. I was getting really depressed about everything too; so I decided one day I'd just give in my notice at the job I was in and go like that, off down to London and have a holiday. I had about £40 altogether in savings and holiday money and back pay, so I asked for my cards, went back to the house, packed a few things in my case, left a note for my mother and step-father, and caught the 'bus to Glasgow and then a coach to London.

I came out at Victoria coach station and went in the first hotel I saw and booked a room there, then I had a few days looking round at all the places like Buckingham Palace and Westminster Abbey that I'd heard about. And would you believe it, in St. Paul's Cathedral I think it was, I walked right into one of the girls who used to be at the factory with me before I got married. She was living down here with her husband but they were separated and she was earning a living as a waitress. She wasn't really a very nice girl, I think; she knocked about a lot with American soldiers and used to go in pubs drinking. Of course I thought she was very daring and exciting, I was easily impressed by all her talk, and when she asked me if I'd like to go to a dance with her one Saturday as a partner for a friend of her friend, I said I would. Both these two men were American soldiers or airmen, I'm not sure which, and me and my friend got separated quite early on in the evening.

I had a lot to drink and felt awful sick and dizzy, and this American gave me something which he said would make me better, he said it was a kind of aspirin. But it just made me worse, I really felt half unconscious with it. He said he knew somewhere where I could sleep it off, and we went to some back street hotel place where we spent the night. In the morning he said he was going out to get a paper, and I waited hours and hours for him but he never came. When I went downstairs the manager said he'd paid the bill and gone straight out, and I thought Well that's funny, it really is, I was quite sure he'd be coming back. His name was Harry, I think.

When I saw my friend again the following day she said he'd probably had to go back to camp in a hurry: she thought it was somewhere up near Cambridge. So I decided I'd go there and see if I could find what had happened to him. When I got to Cambridge on the train someone at the station told me there were a lot of American camps round about, which one was it? I'd no idea at all, so that was the end of it.

I booked in at a hotel in Cambridge because it looked a nice town, and I thought I might have a few days there on holiday. But then I realised I'd hardly any money left at all, not really even enough to pay my hotel bill. I was walking down the street worrying about it late in the afternoon, when I passed an antique shop and I saw a beautiful French clock in the window. So I went in and asked if I could have a look at it, and the manager showed it to me, it was £65.

I said a friend of mine was going abroad, and I'd like to give it her as a present, but my husband wouldn't be back in Cambridge until late that evening—could I possibly take it overnight on approval and show it him and see if he thought it was good enough? I told them the name of the hotel I was staying at, and the manager said that would be quite all right, so out I went with it. Then I walked right over the other side of the town until I saw a second-hand jewellers, and I went in and asked if they bought antiques. They said they did sometimes if they were good enough, so I showed them the clock and said it was my mother's who'd just died and I didn't want it in the house any more.

They said they'd give me £20 for it, and I said that would be fine and took the money, and out I went. I stayed in Cambridge a couple of days, did some shopping with the money, buying a suitcase and some clothes, and then just as I was walking along Trinity Street at lunch-time a police car pulled up and they asked me to go with them to the police station. The hotel had given them my description, I think. I was taken to court and remanded, then I was put up at the Sessions and I got 12 months for it and sent to Holloway.

After I'd been in there a little while I knew there was something wrong with me, so I put down for the doctor and she examined me and told me I was pregnant. I didn't know what to do, whether to write and tell my mother or not, but finally I plucked up my courage and did. There was about three weeks' silence and then I got a letter from her, she said she was really disgusted with me, she said not only being in prison again but being pregnant as well, she thought it was awful. She said I was well old enough to know the difference between right and wrong. It wasn't as though I was too young or anything, and she thought it would be much better if I stayed in the south and had no more to do with her.

I saw the welfare people in prison about the baby and we agreed that I'd have it adopted when it came. But it was such a lovely little boy I didn't want to part with it, I said I was going to keep him. They asked me how I was going to manage outside with him, but I said something would turn up. He was called Michael, and when I left prison he was only a few months old and we were put in a sort of hostel place. I got friendly with a woman there, quite elderly, who'd been left by her husband. She got a flat from the L.C.C., and asked me if I'd like to have a room there with her. I said Oh yes, I would, and went with Michael to her for a while.

She was a very Christian woman, very nice, with a lot of pictures of Jesus up on the walls. She did a lot of praying and grew a beard. She used to come into my room in the dark in the middle of the night, and say 'Don't be afraid, God is in this room.' I got a bit uneasy about it because of the baby, and she started having epileptic fits as well, so I went to live with a lady called Mrs. Robbins who lived in another flat and said I'd be very welcome with her. She had a baby of her own, so I left Michael with her and went to work in a café as a waitress.

This woman Mrs. Robbins whose flat I was living in, I had to pay her £3 a week for my rent and looking after Michael, and it was very hard to do sometimes, especially if I'd been off work with a cold or something like that. I got really fed-up of scraping along living that way.

When I was in Holloway some of the other people there, they'd asked me what I'd done. When I'd told them they said 12 months was an awful lot to get just for a clock that I'd only got £20 for, and if I was going on with that sort of thing, I ought to do it for the sort of money that would make it more worthwhile. So one day I put on my best outfit, and I went off to Regent Street. I looked very nice, very smart, I had a pale blue suit, a big white leather handbag and white shoes, white gloves, and one of those umbrellas with a long straight handle, and my hair all done very nicely in long waves down on my shoulders.

I looked in the windows of the jewellers and the silversmiths: Mappin and Webb's I didn't like the look of, it seemed a bit frightening, but I chose one of the other big ones, and said could I look at some silver tea-services? The man at the counter said what price was I thinking of, and I said it didn't really matter, but I wanted something decent. He put this big piece of velvet on the counter and then he got one set out of a glass case, it was really beautiful, a three-piece one, a Georgian design and figured all over, oh it was lovely. He said it was £195. Then he showed me another one, a four-piece but much plainer and a bit cheaper, I think it was £170; and then there was another one at £230, only I didn't like it, it wasn't anything like so dainty as the Georgian one. So I said to him I liked the £195 one very much, I was very tempted but I didn't know if it was going to be suitable for what I wanted it for, which was for me and my brothers and sisters to give to our parents as a silver wedding present. I said of course they would want to see it first, would it be at all possible to have it on approval for 24 hours? He said he'd have to ask the manager, but he thought it would be all right; and after a few minutes he came back and said it would be all right so long as I could show them some proof of identity. So I said How about my driving licence, would that be all right, he said, of course; then I made a big fuss about having come out without it, but I had an envelope with my name and address on it, and he took a note of that. He packed it up for me very nicely in a box and I said I'd definitely be in the next day, either with the money or bringing it back, but I was quite sure my brothers and sisters would think it was beautiful and we'd keep it.

I hadn't much money on me, and I thought there was no point in going all the way back to the flat with the parcel: I bought a shopping bag off one of the street-sellers in Oxford Street, then I went in a ladies toilet, locked myself in and unpacked the tea-service from the box, and put it in wrapping-paper in the shopping bag. Then I came out, caught a bus along Oxford Street to Marble Arch, and started to walk along the Bayswater Road, quite a long way along to a pawnbrokers and second-hand silver shop I knew was there.

I went in and asked them if they'd like to buy a very good silver tea-service which was in beautiful condition, it'd never been used because it had been given to my parents as a silver-wedding present but they'd been killed in an accident. I took it out of the bag and he said Oh yes, it was really beautiful: he asked me to sit down, and went away in the back somewhere with one piece. I was feeling a bit shaky, wondering if he was going to get in touch with the police or something, but then he came back and said How much did I want for it? I was really very stupid about it, I said Well I'd been thinking of £50. He said Well it was very nice, and in lovely condition, but by the time they'd sold it that was about all they'd get for it themselves, so he could only offer me £45. I let it go for that, I was silly, and he gave me the money all in £5 notes and I signed a receipt for it and gave him my name and address.

I remember coming out and thinking Oh isn't it marvellous, £45—I've got all that money just like that. As I was passing a kiddies'-wear shop I saw a little blue coat with fur on the collar in the window, and I thought That'd just fit my Michael, so I went in and bought it. Then I went into Selfridges and bought a present for the lady who was looking after him for me, one of those lovely vases that change colour as you look at them. Further along Oxford Street again, I went in another shop and bought myself a lovely black skirt: then I thought I'd done enough shopping for one day, and I got on another bus and went straight home to the flat. When Mrs. Robbins saw all the parcels she said 'Have you come into some money then?' and I said well strangely enough I had, just a little bit, and I gave her her present and we put Michael's coat on him; he looked lovely in it.

The next day at work I slipped out and rang up the shop where I'd got the tea service, and I said my brothers and sisters would be deciding that night about it, could I leave coming in till the next day? They said Yes, that would be all right. Well the next day was a Saturday, I didn't ring them up or anything, and all the following week I kept worrying and worrying and wondering what to do. Then one night when I got home from work Mrs. Robbins said two men had been from the shop, and they said they were coming back later. I felt awful about it when they came back. One of them said 'We're not making any accusations against you, Miss McDonald, but please either pay us for the tea service or give it to us back.' I said well I was awfully sorry but I couldn't, and I told them what I'd done with it. Then they said they were very sorry about it but they'd have to tell the police, which they did, and came back again with two C.I.D. men who took me down to the police station and said the best thing would be for me to take them the next morning to the Bayswater Road shop where I'd sold it.

I did that, and then I was put up at Bow Street and remanded to Sessions. While I was in Holloway on remand different detectives kept coming, did I know anything about this that and the other case, would I ask for it to be taken into consideration and so on. They were hoping to get me to admit some that they wanted clearing up, but I wouldn't because I knew nothing about them at all.

When I came to the Sessions the Judge was an old thin-faced one, I've forgotten his name: he said he reckoned I'd done this deliberately and he was going to double what I'd had before, so he gave me two years this time. I didn't have anything to say, just pleaded guilty and I didn't have counsel or anything because there was nothing for him to say either.

Mrs. Robbins said she'd keep Michael and look after him for me, and she had him all the time I was in Holloway. When I came out I didn't really want to go back living with her because of the neighbours, so I got a little room of my own in Acton and went to work in a transport café. After a few weeks one of the drivers who came in regularly and I'd got friendly with said why didn't I get a bigger place, a flat where he could come and have his meals and things, and if I did he'd pay half of it for me although he was living with his stepfather in another flat at the time. I said I would, I'd try to find somewhere, and I did—just a small place, two rooms and a sort of kitchen place. He told me to tell the landlady that he was my husband, and he was a long-distance lorry driver and was away a lot.

He used to come about two or three nights a week, his name was Alf and I really liked him. When I went to see Mrs. Robbins she said You're not going to take Michael to live, are you, I've got so fond of him, so I said Well you can keep him a little while longer if you like. I was paying her £3 a week for him, and £3-10-0 a week for the flat, and I was only earning £8 and Alf wasn't giving me anything for the rent—so all in all, it just wasn't working out and after about three months I was really in a mess again. Alf was talking about us going up to Scotland for a holiday together, and I knew we'd never be able to afford anything like that if the situation didn't improve.

So I thought Well this time I've got to do something really good. I made an appointment to have my hair done, and I put on a very smart black suit I'd got through a catalogue that Mrs. Robbins had, white blouse and white gloves and a little black hat, and off I went up the West End again. It really is a bit exciting, you know, it's like going exploring in a way, setting out on something that you're trying to succeed at, and not knowing what you're going to find.

I tried two big jewellers but they both said they didn't ever let things out on approval, and I was beginning to get depressed, thinking my luck was right out. But the next one was all right, it was a really gorgeous place, it had the Royal crest on the door and carpets that you really sank into when you walked across them. A middle-aged man in a morning suit came up to me, Good morning madam can I help you?

I said I was a teacher at a well-known school, I told him which one, and the staff wanted to give a present to the Headmistress who was retiring, what would he suggest? Had they a very nice silver salver or something like that? He said Yes they had, and he brought several out to show me, including one really big one at £125 with handles on it. I told him I wanted one a bit cheaper because we were getting a tea-service to go on it as well, and finally I chose one at £65. Then he said Had we got the tea-service yet, and I said Well no, actually we hadn't, so he said Could he show me some? There was a very nice one at £135, quite plain, which I liked: I asked him could it have engraving done on it, and he said Oh yes, easily.

Then I said I thought the salver and the tea-service together would be about right, and I'd have to ask the other members of the staff to come in over the next week or two and look at them—unless he could possibly let me have them on approval for a day, could he? He said Yes certainly, of course they could, and he'd have them packed up for me straight away. While that was being done, he saw me looking at a marcasite bracelet at £55. He took it out of the showcase and said would I like to put it on my arm to see how it looked? I said oh yes I would. It was really lovely. I told him I was very tempted by it, I must think about getting it at the end of the month. So he said Why not have it put down on your account, madam? I said well yes, all right, I would. He wrote everything out on a bill, he was going to put it for the school but I said since I'd got the bracelet it'd better all be put down to me at my private address.

He asked should all the things be sent but I said it was all right, one of the other teachers was meeting me for tea at Swan and Edgars and she had her car so we'd manage. So he said Well he would get one of their delivery boys to carry it up to Swan and Edgars for me, which he did. When we got there I told the boy thank you very much, he could just leave me there now: when he was out of sight I got on a 'bus quick, and got off again at a jewellers along Oxford Street.

I went in there and I didn't mention about the silver, only the bracelet which I said I wanted to sell. I told the man a fib, I said it'd cost £65 not £55, and I wanted £45 for it. He said he couldn't manage that, but he'd give me forty, which he did.

Then I got on another 'bus and went home. I didn't unpack the silver, just pushed the parcel under the bed. When Alf came round that evening I told him I'd drawn some money for our holidays and I'd got £40. He said that was marvellous, we'd go very soon; but then the next day he said he couldn't get the time off work, we'd have to wait. I knew it was no good waiting, and I tried to talk him into going for the week-end at least, but he said it couldn't be done because he couldn't afford it unless I drew some more money to see him over.

So that meant I had to go out the next day with the tea-service and the salver, which I'd really wanted to keep a little while. I put them in my shopping bag, and the tea-service I sold down near Victoria for £50 to a little shop where they bought it without any hesitation, just like that: and the salver I took to the silver department of one of the big stores, but they only gave me £42 for it. Still, that was over a hundred pounds in all with the bracelet the day before, and I was quite thrilled about it really.

I went back and told Alf and I said Now we can go to Scotland this week-end. But first I did a lot of shopping, I bought all sorts of things for the flat, masses of tinned food for the larder, everything I needed. Then the next day I thought I'd better 'phone up the shop where I got the silver, just to tell them why they hadn't heard from me—but when I started to explain, the man said 'I'm afraid you're too late, we've put the matter in the hands of the police.' I think they must have got on to the school and found out like that, they were certainly very quick.

I ran straight out of the phone box, I didn't dare go back to the flat, instead I went over to Mrs. Robbins to see Michael, and asked her if I could stop the night there. Next morning when I went into work I felt quite sure something was going to happen, and sure enough round about half past nine two detectives came in for me and took me to the police station. In my handbag there were the bills for the silver marked 'On approval', the receipts for the money from the people I'd sold them too, everything.

So there it was again. Alf came to see me on remand, he was really shocked, he said he'd never have taken money off me if he'd known where I got it from, he thought it was dreadful. When I came up at the Sessions, it was the same Judge again, and he said to me 'You've got no intention of going straight, have you? Well, I doubled it last time, and now I'm going to double it again. This time I'm giving you 4 years. And if you come here any more, you know what you can expect, don't you—8 years, do you understand?'

I went back into Holloway again, and because I'd got a long sentence I had a good clerical job in there that I was more or less permanently on; quite a responsible job it was too. I got it because I'm always so good in prison: in all my time I've never ever once been punished or even put on report for doing anything wrong. A lot of the officers say I'm the very best prisoner they've ever had, because they know I'll give them no trouble at all, and I was so quiet. I didn't mix with the other prisoners, they're not very nice and they use such awful bad language, you wouldn't believe it.

I wrote to my mother again while I was in, asking if I could go back there when I came out, because that's what the welfare thought I ought to do. But she said No, her husband wouldn't be able to stand it, all the worry and that. Alf came to see me and he was very good, he said I could go back with him afterwards and we'd get married; and Mrs. Robbins said she wanted to adopt Michael if only I'd let her. I told the welfare I didn't think she was suitable, she was not very good at keeping herself out of debt and things like that. I said to the welfare I'd really like to go to see my mother on my release, and they were very good, they got me a travel warrant for Glasgow; but I went back to Alf instead, and stopped with him and his step-father for a while.

One night he took me to the pub for a drink, and while we were there Mr. Hardy, who knew Alf, came up and started talking with us, and asked us back here afterwards for some coffee, and put some records on so we could dance. Alf had had rather a bit too much to drink, and he went to sleep in that chair; while he was dancing with me Mr. Hardy said 'He'll never be any good to you, you know, he's no intentions of marrying you. Why don't you come here and look after me, you can walk straight in tomorrow and everything here's yours, you'll have nothing to buy, and we'll get married as soon as my divorce comes through.'

So that was what I did, and I've been here ever since.

* * * * * * *

Talking to Miss McDonald was always an enjoyable experience. We never, of course, reached the familiarity of Christian name terms; and there were certain subjects which were by unspoken agreement only touched-on very briefly, as detailed discussion of them would have been obviously improper.

When she spoke about her visits to the West End shops where she obtained the silver tea-services and the jewellery, her enormous brown eyes seemed to light up, her voice grew firmer and her back straighter; it was as if in re-living the experiences she was becoming a real person and personality in her own right for the first time. And when she described how she chose one tea-service, or one silver salver, rather than another, it was clear from her enthusiasms that what guided her choice was not merely the monetary value: it was personal taste, as though she really *were* choosing the article for a present. Perhaps that was why she was successful, at least in persuading the shop-keepers that she was genuine and could be trusted with the goods on approval: for, incredible though it seems, they really did, as records of her court appearances confirm.

Yet every time she performed her frauds, she ensured disaster for herself by giving her real name and address. Did it never occur to you, I asked once, at least to gain a little time for yourself by giving a made-up name and address? She looked at me in astonishment at the suggestion. Mr. Parker, she said reproachfully and with great dignity, I am not a liar.

On another occasion she mentioned in passing that she was not a thief. What are you then, I asked? Well, she said with quiet reproof, You may think of me what you like, but I have never taken anything from anybody that they didn't willingly give me of their own free will and to my face. I've never stolen from anyone's house, gone in and taken their purse or anything like that, and I've never even shoplifted—I couldn't ever do things which are just stealing, I think it's dreadful.

Could she, I once asked her, think of any reasons why with the kind of background and upbringing which she had had, she could have changed so quickly into someone who indulged in regular criminal activity, and was not put off at all by being caught and repeatedly sent to prison?

Back came the usual answer—'Because I was spoiled I think, as a child, and that made me weak-willed and ....' I asked her not to go on with that, to leave it for the time being, to think and to come back to the subject again another day.

When she did so, her interpretation of her own motives was at least a little less self-condemnatory; but only little more illuminating.

You know you asked me to try and think why I went on and on doing all those things and getting into prison so often? Well one of the reasons I think was that when my husband left me as soon as the baby was born, I wanted to get him back so much I felt if only I could get him to pay some attention to me I'd do anything.

So the first thing I did was to pawn one of his suits; and he just hit me, that was all. Then I went into the Burton's shop and I gave my real name—well, it was his name wasn't it, really—so that I made sure I'd get into trouble. I kept hoping and hoping the first time when I was in prison that he'd feel sorry for me and that he'd left me. I suppose another woman might have started drinking, or going with other men, but I did this instead. I hoped when he heard he'd take pity on me, and start writing to me or come to see me.

But of course it didn't work. It just went on and on, and the more I went into prison the less it seemed to matter to me, the more pushed away from decent people like him and my mother I felt, until in the end I really didn't care at all whether I went into prison or I didn't. Perhaps if I'd been put on probation in the early days, under somebody who could have told me what to do and kept a firm hand over me, that might have worked. To tell you the absolute truth, my mother did go on about it a bit too much, I think, and I don't think it did me much good really.

Do you blame your mother for how you became?

Oh good gracious me no, it wasn't her fault was it? She did her very best for me in every way.

Your husband do you blame at all?

No, no, I don't want to give that impression. You see really and truly I think it was my own fault he left me, because when we got married I wouldn't let him touch me until after the baby was born, I thought it might harm it. I think that was why he went with that blonde lady. Sometimes even now I still think about it all, long ago though it was, twenty years now. If ever I was up there near home and I bumped in to him, I'd have to speak to him . . .

What would you say?

I suppose I'd be stuck for words at first, I'd have to try and say 'Hello' at first, and then to start with I'd ask him how he was getting on and how the boy was. I'd ask him if he was married again or living with anyone else, and if he was happy and being properly looked after; and if . . . and if . . .

And you'd be wanting to say—

Please, please Stanley, will you take me back?

Please forgive me and have me back, I'll try so hard to be good, I really will, if only you'll have me back and give me another chance . . . Oh well, it's all too late to think about now, it's all over and gone. I heard once a few years ago that he'd married that blonde lady, so I suppose that's it.

* * * * * * *

Miss McDonald, since that first time you went into hospital for the electric-shock treatment, have you ever had any further psychological or psychiatric examination or treatment, either while you've been remanded in custody before sentence or during the long periods you've spent in prison?

Oh no, there's been nothing like that, I've never needed it, you see. That shock treatment was because I'd got so depressed and unhappy at that time, but I've never had that trouble again. I'm a very happy person, and always have been ever since—because I think on the whole I've been very lucky and had a good life and an enjoyable one.

All the prison doctors who've ever examined me have all said the same thing, that I'm a fine, fit, healthy woman and there's nothing wrong with me at all, and no reason for me to go on getting into trouble either— except that I'm weak-willed because I was spoiled so much when I was a child.

I mean, I can't say it was anyone else's fault at all except mine, can I? I've always got myself into trouble, no one else has led me into it. After all, nobody makes you do things, do they, except yourself?

Did you say you thought you'd been lucky and had a good and enjoyable life?

Yes I do, and I have—everything provided for me always right from being a child, a good mother, a nice home. Of course going to prison wasn't so nice, because you meet so many rough types of person there. And if I get sent there again—well, next time that old Judge said it'd be Preventive Detention for me, so let's hope it doesn't ever come to that, eh?

JANIE PRESTON

LARCENY

AGE: *60*
NUMBER OF CONVICTIONS: *16*
TOTAL TIME SPENT IN PRISON: *12 years 2 months*

V

Janie Preston

PREVENTIVE DETENTION, in the form introduced by the 1948 Criminal Justice Act, was intended to deal with 'persistent offenders who by their age, criminal history and character, seem to be beyond correction and can be restrained only by prolonged detention'. (*Prisons & Borstals: Statement of Policy and Practice. Home Office*, 1960.) The sentence—which might be for any period between five and fourteen years, depending on how the Judge was feeling—could be given only to offenders over 30 years of age who had been in prison at least twice before: and 'it is of the essence of the system that the offender is not being punished for the last offence of which he was convicted, but is confined for the protection of society and for a period which is likely to exceed any period for which he could have been imprisoned as a punishment.' (*Ibid.*)

In addition, though the motive was never publicly stated, there was also the underlying hope that fear of receiving Preventive Detention might deter 'professional' criminals from continuing their life of crime. Advocates of the necessity for retaining the sentence in the penal code argued that no one could tell just how many had been so deterred. But what could be seen, and seen the more clearly the longer it remained, was that it was not often being received by 'professionals': it fell most frequently on offenders with long records of petty crime, among whose many social inadequacies was their inability to avoid capture. For that type of offender it was the least condign of all punishments.

Based on false premises, ill-considered, inept in its application, costly to the community and cruel though Preventive Detention was, the credit (if that is the correct word) for devising it is claimed for the former Director of Prisons, Sir Alexander Paterson (1884-1947) by the editor of his posthumous papers who describes it as 'One of the theories of penology which he evolved during his career at the Home Office. He was well aware that some men are incorrigible, and believed that society should be given the maximum protection from such men.'

Paterson had written: 'There will always remain a residuum of habitual criminals who have resisted or evaded all efforts to train them for honest life. By weakness of character or wilful defiance of society's axioms they have shown themselves unfit for freedom. "Training" in their case is likely to be a misuse of the word and a waste of time. The exact period which they should spend in prison should not be determined entirely by the gravity of the offence, but by their fitness for the resumption of social life.'

(He also wrote, on another occasion: 'We should accept with caution the findings of psychologists, and rely rather on deduction from the fundamental principles we accept'; and other ideas of his were that both corporal and capital punishment were necessary, the latter on the grounds that it was more 'merciful' than imprisonment. But it was also Sir Alexander Paterson who first stated the now often-quoted dictum 'Men come to prison *as* a punishment, not *for* punishment.' He was that curious but not-uncommon mixture of insight and obtuseness and humaneness and severity which a combination of Christianity, private-school education, and service in the armed forces so steadily reproduces in order that the Prison Department of the Home Office may perpetuate itself without intercourse.)

A recommendation that Preventive Detention should be abolished was made by a Government-appointed Advisory Council on the Treatment of Offenders in its report in 1963. But the Council suggested that in place of it courts should be given power to pass longer sentences of ordinary imprisonment on persistent offenders, thus abolishing a name but making no fundamental alteration of the legal approach to the problem. Government action in 1963 gave effect to the first of these recommendations.

It remains to be seen whether judges will ever be bold enough to refrain from passing sentence of *any* kind of imprisonment on petty criminals already grossly institutionalised by the amount of time they have spent inside, and try instead to find some alternative treatment which might revitalize, instead of confirm the destruction of, the offender's personality. They have the power to do it.

'The Crown Courts', wrote Judge Neville Laski in The Liverpool Daily Post in 1963 'enable the Judge to be untrammelled by the calendar and to indulge to the full in pre-sentence enquiry. I can conscientiously say that I have never dealt in terms of Preventive Detention or any lengthy sentence unless I had a full personal report on the man or woman concerned, or knew them from previous unhappy contact.'

The reports to which he refers are those made by

the Home Office on the convicted prisoner. Unless an After-Care agency goes out of its way to offer information, they deal almost exclusively with previous offences and convictions, in order to inform the Judge of the prisoner's 'suitability' (that is, *legal eligibility*) for a long sentence. When such prisoners appear in court, one of their characteristics is that they almost invariably plead 'Guilty' and offer no defence; they are therefore not given Legal Aid and are unrepresented. On average less than ten minutes is devoted to each case: most of this time is taken-up by Prosecuting Counsel outlining the accused's offence, followed by a police officer recounting the previous criminal history, to whom 'Just the last three convictions, officer' is the invariable instruction from the Judge. The accused is asked if he has anything to say by way of explanation of his behaviour. Not unnaturally he usually has little to contribute. He is then sentenced.

In the eyes of the Law the fact that the offender has been properly and correctly found 'Guilty' is all that matters. It is assumed—unless he is so grossly mentally disturbed that even the Court Usher can diagnose it—that the reason he continues to get into trouble is because he is either wicked or weak; and that he can only be changed by being taught a lesson. If he refuses to learn the lesson, punishment must be increased until he does; and it is finally in order 'to protect society' that the persistent offender is given either Preventive Detention or a long term of imprisonment. It is as if a doctor were to examine every patient who comes to his surgery; pronounce them all 'Ill'; and prescribe for them all the same medicine.

Women preventive detainees are much less numerous than men. In the last ten years only about fifty have served such a sentence. This is the story of one of them,

Janie Preston, whose record over the past 30 years is this:—

Age 18—2 years' Probation for larceny
Age 19—6 months' hard labour for larceny
Age 20—Bound over for 12 months for larceny
ditto   —12 months for larceny of £20
Age 25—Bound over for 12 months for larceny

Age 34—6 months for larceny of £30
Age 35—4 months for larceny
Age 37—8 months for larceny
Age 38—Bound over for 2 years for larceny

Age 40—15 months for larceny
Age 42—3 months for stealing a skirt
Age 44—6 months for stealing £3 in an hotel
Age 48—Fined £10 for larceny
Age 49—6 months for larceny
Age 50—2 years for larceny of £20

Her next sentence was 8 years' Preventive Detention, after a further offence of larceny involving £55. It was given to her when she was 52, at Liverpool Assizes by Judge Neville Laski.

* * * * * * *

I first met her two years ago, on the day after she had been released from prison. There had been a change in penal administration: all preventive detainees had suddenly been given one-third remission of sentence, instead of the one-sixth which most of them until then had usually received. As a result five women who had already served more than two-thirds of their time were unexpectedly released. Janie was one of them.

She had been inside for over six years, was unprepared for freedom, and it meant not happiness for her, but terror. She begged to be given a job, any job, inside the prison and not be turned-out until her full sentence was completed, rather than have to go out into a world where she knew no one, had nowhere to live, no job, no roots, no security. The plea was useless: the regulations had been changed, and she and the four others had to be discharged immediately.

A stout ugly unhappy old woman, she put her hands down dejectedly on the edge of the table in the room we were talking in, put her face down on her hands, and wept. Bitterly and unceasingly, she poured out her Lancashire-accented threnody; unhesitatingly, because she could tell me about it, I'd understand her, I'd know what it was like, because I had a Lancashire accent too . . .

Why musta come out, why musta, can you tell me that? Why couldn'ta stay where I was? I wasn't doin' no 'arm, was a, I'd done nothin' wrong in there, I didn't ask ter come out, did a? Why couldn't they just've left me alone? I don't want to be outside, I don't want to be, I just want to be back where a belong in me cell.

I'll never pick up again outside, never a won't, not now, a can't. Not after six year in there, I'll never do it, it can't be done. In prison you're left on your own so much, you're locked up in your cell for hours and hours on end; you can't just come out and be free, you can't, it's terrible, you can't.

They give me a room last night that they'd found for me, a room in a little boarding-house round at the back of Waterloo. They took me there and left me, they said 'You'll be all right here for tonight now Janie, it's a nice little room with clean sheets on the bed and a dressing table, you'll be all right now Janie, you'll be fine . . . '

After they'd gone I just lay on the bed, I just lay there and lay there, waiting for someone to come along the landing and turn the light off outside the door, like they do in prison. All today I've been asking people what time it is, even though I've got my own watch back on again. I've been touching my clothes and wondering where they've come from, because I've forgotten them; they're the ones I had on when I went in. And I've kept feeling my hat on my head to see if it's still there . . .

I'll never get used to it. Why have a got to? I hate outside. Why must a be pushed out all of a sudden like this, why, why?

She had no friends; nor, she said flatly on that first day, did she want any. She didn't want to have anything to do with other people, she just wanted to be left on her own. Nobody liked her, she knew that; there was nothing likeable about her, she'd always known. She was like an animal trapped in a cage of misery and loneliness, pacing up and down in it, ready to scratch and slash and spit at anyone who tried to get near the bars.

* * * * * * *

Eight months later, I met Janie again. She was by then the only surviving member of the quintet of women who had been released together. Of the others two had died, and two had been reconvicted and sent back to prison.

How did it feel to be the only one left? Without any pretence at concern for the others, without even a moment's thought for them, she said Oh it's absolutely smashing, I'm thrilled to be the only one who's still here.

And no one ever thought I'd make it did they, she said. No one thought I'd stay out—you didn't yourself, did you?

No, I said, I didn't. No said Janie, I knew you didn't: and neither did I.

She had been lucky. After a few unsuccessful attempts at work, first as a waitress and then as a shop assistant, and walking out from each job after a few days in a temper, she had been wandering round the north London streets one day when a 6d.-a-week advertisement on a postcard in a glass case outside a newspaper shop caught her eye. 'Wanted: Middle-aged housekeeper to look after elderly invalid. Live in'.

The address was nearby. At the house she was welcomed by an anxious woman whose desperate concern was to find someone to look after her eighty-two year old father, while she and her husband went for six months on a business trip to South Africa. Two women had been tried already; they had both left after only twenty-four hours because her father swore at them.

All that would be required, she said, would be for Janie to give the old man his breakfast at nine, his dinner at twelve-thirty, and his tea at four. For the rest of the day he wanted to be left alone in his library with his books, and he went to bed at about seven o'clock every evening. There was a basement flat for the housekeeper to live in: when the old man wanted his meals he would thump on the floor with his stick. If he was ever ill, send for the doctor, who knew him well. Three pounds a week plus housekeeping money and, of course, the little flat downstairs. The two big things were, said the woman, that her father didn't like any company and wanted to be left alone: and he sometimes used very bad language.

Janie sniffed; she thought she could put up with

that, she said: she'd give it a try. The only other thing was, said the woman—she hated to ask this, but she and her husband were due to sail the very next day—could Janie possibly move in that same afternoon? She thought it could be managed, said Janie: she'd have to go home to her family and explain why it was so quick but it would probably be all right. The two previous nights she had in fact spent sleeping on benches at railway stations: Victoria one, Waterloo the other. She had a total of 4½d. in her pocket, and her suitcase of clothing was in the left-luggage at Waterloo.

By the end of that afternoon she was in the warmth and comfort of the basement flat. It had its own kitchen, a television set in the sitting-room; and upstairs the elderly recluse who had to be fed three times a day and otherwise left alone. Probably he wouldn't live long, and probably she would soon be out of the place and wandering the streets again. But in the meantime, she might as well make the most of it.

* * * * * * *

I continued to see her. The months went by, and the old man upstairs remained alive and went on thumping on the floor three times a day for his meals. In the basement flat underneath Janie sat and knitted, or watched the television. Every day she went down to the shops at the bottom of the road for the small amounts of food necessary for the two of them. Sometimes on the way home she slipped into the pub on the corner for a quick Guinness, then hurried back to prepare the next meal.

She cut out a picture of lakes and mountains in Switzerland from a magazine, and stuck it on the wall of her bed-sitting room. In time it was joined by others: a spaniel, a television announcer, the cast of 'Emergency—Ward 10', and a coloured photograph of a chef's table piled high with a decorative arrangement of the ingredients needed for *bouillabaisse*. She bought a wireless and sent up a postal order for five shillings to the Radio Caroline Club; she planted two hyacinth bulbs in fibre in a bowl, and they grew. The old man's daughter and her husband returned from South Africa and decided to leave things as they were for the time being. Janie bought herself a morning-tea set, slowly knitted herself a green woollen dress, then a bright purple one.

Whenever I saw her, there was really only one subject of conversation: prison. One-third of her adult life had been spent there: she had been inside so often and so long that it made up nearly the whole fabric of her personality. (Diane too had been unable to discuss much else at first, but she had talked mainly about the people there, whereas Janie's conversation was entirely about places—how the food in Holloway was better than the food in Manchester, and the food in Exeter better than either of them; how Durham was rough, Cardiff was easy, and Birmingham was not so nice.)

She was unused to talking about herself, and uneasy about it, and would sit taut and upright on the settee, her hands clenched tightly together in her lap and her slate-grey eyes hooded and hidden behind her glasses, until she was sure she was not under attack. A big, forbidding-looking woman, with black hair, a deeply-lined face, and a thin-lipped and twisted mouth.

As time went on and we came to know each other better, it was possible gradually to reduce the confused jumble of prisons and sentences to some sort of order; even occasionally to move away from the subjects altogether, and talk instead of her life before it became such a dreary and meaningless pattern of crime and punishment and crime. But it was always difficult for both of us; her memory was fragmented and her sense of chronology defective. Sometimes only a comma between two phrases would mark the ellipsis of nearly fifty years—'I was always terribly quick-tempered as a girl, I was punished five times on my last sentence for swearing at the officers.'

And when she talked, it was with all the directness and openness of a Lancastrian, used as a camouflage to conceal the secret and unspeakable hurt beneath.

When we met that first day after you'd come out of prison, you said you'd no friends and you didn't want any. Have you made any friends since you've come out?

No, not one. I haven't tried to and I'm not going to. I stay in my room here and I don't want any friends, I can do all right without them, thanks.

Have you always been like this, or did you have friends when you were younger?

Always. I told you before, I don't like people and I never have. They've not liked me either, so we're quits. Ever since being a girl I've wanted to keep myself to myself and not have nothing to do with no one. When I was younger I always had the idea I'd like to live right out of the way on top of a mountain—somewhere like in that picture I've stuck on the wall there. Or on the top of Shap Fell, somewhere like that. I've been up over Shap two or three times. Do you know it? There's a few houses up there, aren't there, and I've always felt that's where I'd like to be, up there on my own away from everybody. I often used to wish I'd been born a man instead of a woman; and then if I had I could have got a job as a long-distance lorry driver, so I could always have been moving, on and on and on, driving for ever and ever away from people.

Why?

I don't know why, I've just felt like it as long as I can remember, that's all. I don't like people: it's as simple as that.

Who have you ever liked in your life?

No one.

Your mother and father?

Not really, no. There was an officer in Durham when I was there on remand, she said to me once 'You know what's wrong with you, Preston, is that you like no one, no one likes you, and you're proud of it.' I said 'Well there's nothing wrong with that, that's just how I like it, and you can mind your own bloody business.'

You wouldn't have been allowed to answer an officer back like that in the old days when I first went in: it was much stricter than it is now. All the prisons were a lot harder then, and I think it was better in a way too, because you knew what prison was for; it was to punish you and then let you out when you'd finished, none of this trying to reform people all the time.

I was about eighteen, I think, the first time I went in. I was taken to Strangeways and put in this big room with all the little cubicles along the side of it. You had to go in one and take all your clothes off, and they gave you a rough kind of dressing-gown thing and took all your clothes away. That first time, I thought it was what prison was going to be, spending all my time in the cubicle with only this dressing-gown to wear. Then they gave you a lump of bread and some margarine and a mug of cocoa, and then they took you for your bath. After that you went and saw the doctor. In Strangeways in those days she used to make you get up on two chairs with your legs wide apart, one foot on each, and then jump off on to the floor. You had to do it three times, to make sure you weren't concealing anything.

I had hard labour—and it was hard labour too. You had to walk everywhere in single file and you weren't allowed to talk. Number 1 labour I was doing; that was outside in the prison yard. You stood in a long line down one side of some big trestle-tables with sheets of metal on them. Then the men came from the men's part of the prison, they had wheelbarrows full of rock which they tipped out on the tables for you. We had to get out the hard lumps and bash the other rocks to bits; then the bits were shovelled along to a stone slab at the end, and there they had to be ground down with other lumps of stone into a fine powder. Then you had to sweep the powder off into barrows, and wheel it over to the storerooms. I think it was sandstone, and it was made up into blocks, they were called 'Donkey stones' that people used for whitening steps with and cleaning stone floors.

I got big segs on my hands after a time, it was better when your hands were harder, then you got used to it. They were very strict in those days; we got up at half past six, tidied our cells, then went and did an hour's work till eight; then we had breakfast, then we had school till 10 o'clock, then we worked till twelve, had our dinner, and worked again until four o'clock.

One time when I was in the sewing machine shop at Strangeways Manchester one of the officers, Miss Bishop, she's retired now, she said 'Preston, do you know that old hut on the croft round the back of Deansgate? When I leave the prison service I'm going to rent that for my girls, I'm going to have a sewing factory there, and you can come and work for me.'

I wonder if she ever did? It was a good idea. She told me to enquire at the gate of the prison if I ever went up there again, to see if she'd done it. They used to call for her when I was up in my cell crying before I came out, they'd send her to see me and have a talk with me and try and get me to agree to go out, because I never wanted to go. That's what she used to say to calm me down—'One day Preston you can come and work for me.' I expect she'll be dead by now, Miss Bishop.

They could have done with a few like her in Holloway, I didn't like that place, it wasn't a proper prison at all. P.D.'s, C.T.'s, Y.P.'s (Preventive Detainees, Corrective Trainees, Young Prisoners) all mixed up together, it was horrible. And some of those young ones, Borstal girls who'd run away and been recaptured, oh they were terrible—noisy, rowdy, thought they were really tough because they were in the nick. There was only one person in Holloway I ever talked to much at all; that was the Salvation Army woman. She found out one day I'd been in the Salvation Army when I was young, so she used to come up to my cell and talk to me about it sometimes.

How old were you when you were in the Salvation Army?
I'd be about nineteen or twenty, I suppose.
How did you come to join it?
Well I didn't actually join it, I was put in one of their hostels instead of being sent to prison. I was on probation or bound over on condition I went there, something like that. I was drinking a lot at the time as usual, and they thought the Salvation Army might cure me of it, because they're all teetotal, and they have a big thing about saving people from the evils of drink, don't they? But one day I had a row with them and left. I went through every room in the place first, every coat and jacket and handbag I could find, and got about seven pounds altogether, I think.
You were doing a lot of drinking, you say, at nineteen?
I've always been a big drinker, dear, whenever I could get it. Not now since I've come out, because

being inside for so long and having to do without it I've got out of the habit. Anyway, I can't do it much while I'm living here, because there's his meals to be got. But if I ever had to leave here and start wandering again, well that's what I'd be doing all right, there's no doubt about that.

Before when I was out, I was always in the pubs, from 11 o'clock until three o'clock, and from there to a club if I could find one until 6 o'clock, then straight back in the pub at 6 o'clock until eleven. But I wouldn't let anybody else buy me a drink, I always bought my own unless I was after somebody's money.

What I mean is, if ever a chap came in the pub like some of these men do, on their own and want to get friendly with everyone, well they stand at the bar and take out a roll of notes to show they've got plenty. And then if they see a woman on her own they offer to buy her a drink, don't they? When someone like that came in, a mug ready for plucking, well I'd have him. He could buy me a drink, two drinks if he wanted —and I'd guarantee before ten minutes I'd have his money and away. It's not difficult picking men's pockets if you're a woman; usually it's them that wants to get close to you, they start pushing theirselves near you. As soon as you've got their wallet or their purse or whatever it is, 'Excuse me' you say, 'I won't be a moment' and off you go with it. They'd never think of following you because they think you're going to the toilet, don't they?

I had nearly twenty pounds off a man once, he had it all in one pound notes in his wallet. I took it out and hid it under a slab of concrete down near a railway bridge, in case the police picked me up with it while I was wandering round. I used to go back every night and get a few pounds out to spend on my beer.

Is this when you were in your twenties or thirties or forties, when was it?

That particular time would be when I was about thirty, I should think. It's a bit difficult for me to get it all in order; I've been pinching money since right back in the early days, and getting caught all the time and going to prison for it. One part of my life wasn't much different from another, that's the trouble: I don't know if you'll ever be able to sort it all out . . .

My mother had thirteen children and I was the eldest. She was very young when she had me, only just over sixteen. My dad was very young too, he was only about sixteen as well. He worked in the pits; I don't think he can have been much good to her because she chucked him about four years after I was born, and married a soldier from the barracks at Ardwick. There was me and my sister she had from my father, then all the others she had from my step-father. We all called him 'Dad', he was more like our real father—when he was there, which wasn't a lot, because after a bit the Great War started and he went to France. My mum was carrying on while he was away with this man and that man, oh there were dozens of them. I shouldn't think anybody ever knew who were who's children; she was awful.

I was about nine when the war started; I don't remember a lot about it except seeing soldiers everywhere and big posters with that man on with a moustache, pointing his finger out and saying, 'We want YOU.' I used to think he meant me.

We lived just outside Manchester in one of those terraced houses like you see rows and rows of in the north. Well really we lived in two of them, because next door to our house was my grandmother and grandfather's house, and my mother had so many kids some of us lived with them, including me. The sofa in the front room of my grandma's, that was my bed for as long as I can remember, I always slept there. My grandpa had the corner grocer's shop, when we were kids we used to like it when he let us help him behind the counter, weighing out pennyworths of sweets for the other kids that came in.

I think I was quite happy as a child, I know my grandmother brought us up mostly, and was always rowing with my mother about these men she used to bring back to the house. I got ill once when I was young and had to go into hospital: I don't know what it was I had, but I know it meant I couldn't ever have any children when I grew up. My granny told me about it at the time, that that was what it would mean. I seemed to get the idea she was putting the blame on my mother for it somehow, though I never found out why.

When the war was over I remember my step father coming back in his soldier's uniform, but he didn't live with us, he soon went somewhere else and there was no man living at home at all, just a lot of these 'uncles' who kept coming. One of them was a very good-looking young chap called Mike. I met him one morning in the cemetery I used to walk through on my way to school. He was sitting on a bench there. He asked me if I'd like to go to the pictures with him and I said, Yes, I would. I thought I was really grown up, didn't I, not yet thirteen and already getting a boy-friend asking me to go to the pictures with him?

But when I got home from school in the afternoon my mum was waiting for me, and she said 'I was watching you out of the upstairs back window this morning: I saw you talking to that man in the cemetery, what did he want?' I said 'It's not *that man,* it was me uncle Mike and he wants me to go to the pictures with him.' So my Mum said 'Well you're not going' and I said 'Oh you're just jealous, that's all you are.' But she wouldn't let me have any more to do with him, she said I wasn't to walk through the cemetery in the mornings on my way to school either, and so that was the end of that.

Not long after, when I was about 14 I left school and went to work in the mill, and I was earning about fifteen shillings a week which was quite a lot of money in those days. My mum and my grandmother between them used to take twelve and six a week off me, so if ever I saw any money lying around at home I used to take it and hide it in a stocking inside the back of the sofa in my grandmother's front room. My younger sister, she could always get money for spending off my mother; and she was let stay out till all hours too, she was really spoiled. I was working and yet they treated me as if I was younger than she was, always giving her things and letting her do what she liked.

One day I came home and the stocking with the money in it had gone from the back of the sofa. I couldn't say anything about it, could I, because I wasn't supposed to have the money anyway. But I saw my sister looking at me and trying not to laugh, so it was obvious who'd had it, wasn't it? I got my own back a few years later, I walked in the house one day and there was her handbag on the kitchen table, it had about four quid in it and I had that. I still laugh, I don't know if she's any idea to this day where it went.

I worked at the mill for about a year, and then I gave up because I didn't see any point in going on working for money I had to give to my mother when I got home; especially as I'd found out by then that money came a lot easier when you pinched it instead of working for it. Most people left their back doors open in the north, and you could just go in anytime you liked to people's houses. They all used to have bits of money lying about, in jam jars on shelves, in cocoa tins on the mantelpiece, places like that. I'd knock on the back door and if there was no one there, in I'd go.

What I wanted the money for, of course, was beer, because by the time I was 16 I'd developed a proper taste for it. I first had some in a pub where I'd been sent with a jug to get it for my grandpa; I drank some on the way home, then filled the jug up with water in the kitchen. I got into the habit of doing that, then I had to have some of my own, and that's how it started.

I used to walk about for days at a time, in the pubs until I'd got no more money, then off down the road going in houses until I'd got a few shillings, then on to the next pub and so on. I went to Lancaster, Fleetwood, Blackpool, New Brighton—all over the place, always filthy dirty and just wandering about stealing and drinking and sleeping rough. The tram shelters on Blackpool promenade, the Ribble bus garage at Bolton, the railway sidings at Oldham—I've slept in them all in my time, in fact I always used to say I could sleep better rough than I could in a bed.

Now and again I used to go to big houses and ask them did they want a maid? If they said Yes I'd move in, and then out again in a few days after I'd helped myself to any money they left lying around. I never took anything else but money; and as soon as I got it, straight down to the pub until it was all gone. Of course it couldn't go on, could it? Sure enough I had to get caught, and I did. All the money I'd took, and I got caught taking half-a-crown off the kitchen mantelpiece in a big house that belonged to a chief constable, of all people!

They put me on probation for that. Not that it made any difference; I went straight off to the next town and carried on drinking and stealing there. Only a few weeks went by before I was caught again in another house—and this time I was sent to prison for six month's hard labour.

When I came out, on I went again with the wandering round and the drinking straight away. I turned up at home once in the middle of the night I remember, and got into the cellar and slept on the coal. My mother came screaming and yelling at me in the morning, told me to get out and not come back no more, said I was a dirty filthy thing and she didn't want to see me ever again.

Another time I remember I got in a garage, I think it was in Rochdale or somewhere like that. I went to sleep in the back of a car, and in the morning when I woke up I stepped straight out into a big pan of dirty black oil that was on the floor. I was trying to wipe it off myself when they came and opened up the place. When they saw me they sent for the police. But I wasn't doing anything, only sleeping in the back of a car, so the police just told me to move on.

I looked like a bundle of old rags most times, you couldn't have told whether I was a boy or a girl or an old man or an old woman or what. Now and again someone would offer me a square meal and I'd say I'd sooner have the money, and as soon as I got it I was into the nearest pub. There were men of course who'd offer me money if I'd go with them, but I'd never let them anywhere near me, the dirty beasts. I used to swear at them and tell them to go off and find themselves a tart if they wanted that sort of thing. Then they'd come over all apologetic, wouldn't they, and say they were sorry, and perhaps give me ten bob because

I was shouting to quieten me down. It was an easy way of getting a few bob, to let them go on until they made their improper suggestion, and then start screaming about it.

All in all, that kind of life has been the only kind of life I've ever led—wandering round, thieving, drinking, going into prison, coming out and wandering round again. There was one period in my life where if you look at my record, it shows nearly ten years that I had between the ages of twenty-five and thirty-four without any convictions. Sometimes people say, like a Judge or someone in prison who's doing welfare, 'Well Janie, you kept out of trouble once for nearly ten years, why can't you do it again?'

Yet you know in all that time I wasn't leading a different kind of life. I don't think there was one day when I mightn't have been picked-up and sent to prison, if I'd been unlucky and it'd just happened like that. It certainly wasn't that I was going straight or anything; only that I wasn't being caught.

At one time round about then, for about a year in fact, I was friendly with a police Inspector who knew me very well because he was always in and out of the pubs that I was in. He never nicked me once. I think I was too valuable to him in letting him know what was going on round the town. He told his men to lay off me altogether—so that helped as well as far as not getting into trouble with the Law was concerned, too.

I got married once. That was funny it was; well not funny it was stupid, really. I was forty-five, forty-six perhaps, and I met this middle-aged chap in a pub one night, he was telling me all his life story about how his wife had died and all the rest of it. A couple of nights later I ran into him again in a different pub. He seemed all right, he was prepared to buy beer for me without thinking he was buying me at the same time, no messing about with his hands or anything like that, and after I'd met him about six or seven times he suddenly blurted out 'What would you say if I asked you to marry me?'

I wasn't really bothered one way or the other, was I, so long as I had my beer. He'd got a nice big house nearby that he took me to see, so that was how it happened. It lasted three weeks and then he took me to court for going after him with a chopper—one of those big meat choppers it was, I used to keep it in the top of the gas oven and take it out and threaten him with it if he ever tried to put his hands on me.

I would have too, I'd have killed him if he'd come near me. I said 'I've married you for my beer money, and I don't want any of that other business.' So he took me to court and the police came back home with me afterwards, and I had to give them the chopper. Anyway I left the house soon after that, so that was the end of him. I can't stand men mauling and messing you about, their hands all over you—ugh, no thanks, they can find someone else if they want that.

The next time I was in prison after that, I'd got six months I think it was, and I got the papers from some solicitors to say he was divorcing me, so it was good riddance to bad rubbish, I was better off where I was.

Then I got two years, didn't I, what was that for? Oh it was Woolworth's, I think, following the girl round who was emptying the tills one lunch-time. She put all the money in a bag, a hold-all thing, and when she got to the office she put it down on the floor while she unlocked the door. I put my hand in and ran off with a handful of notes but they came after me and caught me. Yes, two years I got for that, that's right.

It wasn't long after I came out from that one that I

got my eight years in Liverpool. I'd been out about three or four months I think, and I was in a pub one day at Southport. I asked the publican if I could use his telephone behind the bar and he said Yes. Then as I was coming away from the counter I put my hand in his till and took a lot of notes, fifty-five pounds there was altogether, and out I went. But I made the mistake of going back in the same pub again about two weeks later, and the landlord recognised me and called the police.

Judge Laski said 'How many convictions has she got altogether?' and somebody said 'Fifteen'. He said 'All for things like this?' and they said 'Yes'. He said to me 'Well it's terrible' he said, 'Really shocking. Have you got anything to say for yourself?' I said No: well there wasn't anything *to* say, was there? So he said 'We shall have to keep you apart from the public, you're a menace, there's no doubt about that. I'm going to send you to Preventative Detention for eight years.'

I thought Well, that's it then, I'm all right, I've got nothing else to worry about now for eight years. I did the first part of it in Strangeways, then they sent me down to Holloway. I had the best cell in the prison, right up on the top floor at the end of the block it was. After they'd locked me in of a summer evening, I could climb up on my chair and look out of the window, and I could see right down to the front gate, over the wall to the road opposite, and away over all the roofs right as far as King's Cross nearly, it was smashing. No one ever came up to bother you, I was right on my own completely.

Then it had to come to a finish, and I had to come out. But if *this* comes to an end, and I have to leave here and start wandering again, when I go back inside I'm going to try and get my own cell back.

Prison holds no terrors for you, does it?

Terrors? No, why should it, I don't mind being inside. Once you're in there you're safe, aren't you?

Safe from what?

Well, I mean you can't do no more harm, can you, you can't do anything else wrong in prison? I ought to have been in for life, then I'd have been really happy.

Do you think it might have made a difference to you if you'd been treated differently when you first got into trouble—if they'd persevered with your probation, perhaps?

No I don't think so. I don't see how they could have done, anyway—they had to send me to prison, didn't they?

If you did something now that you got caught for, and the Judge decided not to send you back again, how would you feel?

I'd think he'd gone potty, wouldn't I? He'd have to send me back for another very long time, he couldn't do anything else.

You don't think there's any other way of treating habitual offenders like you?

No, of course there isn't; after all, we've done wrong, haven't we, and we've got to be punished for it. Unless . . . oh well, they don't do it now, so what's the use.

What were you going to say?

Well, I was going to say that another thing might be to do what they did in the old days, and deport the criminals.

Do you think you ought to have been deported?

I used to, yes, when I was younger.

Where to?

Java.

Java? Why Java?

I saw some pictures of it once, years ago it was now, long before the war, in a magazine, and I thought Yes, that's where I ought to be sent to work, amongst those people.

What people were they?

It was a leper colony, it showed you pictures of them all with leprosy, their hands, their fingers, their noses. They were all disfigured, eaten away, lying on the ground. I thought if they could send me out there and I could work among people like that, that'd be the place for me.

* * * * * * *

Throughout our conversations over a period of more than a year, Janie's fundamental attitudes and outlook never changed. Prison was where she belonged; she wanted to be there because she couldn't stand people; no one could ever possibly like her, and so she would never like anyone else. She ought to be in prison; she deserved to be punished; she was guilty; she was bad. She said this kind of thing repeatedly, never self-pityingly but as a kind of catechism she had learned from when she was a child.

Not being a psychotherapist I felt I had no justification for probing too deeply into the subject, merely to confirm my own theories about what lay under an attitude of this kind, mixed so obviously and inextricably as it was with a profound distaste for sex. Sometimes when we were discussing motives for behaviour a frightened and hunted look would come into her eyes, her hands would begin to twine desperately together and she was never at ease until the conversation was back again on the safe lines of prison routine or the comparative virtues and failings of different governors.

Yet often equally obviously she was trying to find an opportunity to say something which was troubling her a great deal. 'You see' she would begin, 'there's one thing connected with it which I've never told anybody

. . . Nobody knows about it, there's nobody living now who knows about it except me, all the other people who had to do with it are dead.' Then her voice would lose its strength, she would grimace, shrug, say 'Oh well I don't suppose it's got anything to do with it, really' and go on to another subject. Even on the occasion when she came out with the startlingly plain placing of herself in the leper-colony in Java, the subsequent questions and answers led rapidly away from the point again:—

Have you ever wanted to work with anyone else besides lepers?

No.

Lepers are social outcasts, aren't they, or used to be. Why do you associate yourself with them?

I don't know.

Have you always felt you were a social outcast?

Yes, but I don't know why. There was an officer in Manchester once, she said to me 'There's lots of other people worse off than you, Preston, what about the starving families in Africa?' I said 'Oh bugger them, what about the starving families in this prison, did you see what they gave us for our dinner today?' The food in there it was terrible, it really was, they used to give us potatoes that were all black and maggoty, the bread was mouldy, the tea was . . .

When it did come at last, it came straight and without much prompting. What it must have cost her eventually to say it is beyond calculation.

Will you have another bun?

No thank you I've had three.

What's the matter, don't you like them? I made them specially for you coming because you said you liked anything with currants in.

I like them very much but——

Have another one then and do as you're told, I don't want them all to waste do I?

All right, just one. I'll never be able to eat any supper when I get home though.

Go on, you could do with eating more, you look as though you need some weight on, you smoke too much and eat too little.

Probably. Can I just ask you one or two more questions before we finish for this afternoon?

Yes, go on. Wait till you've finished your bun though, I can't tell what you say.

Right: it's true to say, isn't it, that you've never had the slightest compunction ever about stealing—you've always taken money because you felt you had a right to?

Yes.

Why did you feel that?

I don't know. I've told you about my sister taking the stocking I kept in the settee, and then getting my own back on her; but I'm not saying I always stole to get my own back on my sister or anything like that.

Why did you steal, have you any idea?

No.

Whenever you were found out, you always got into trouble for it. Did you mind being found out?

No.

I sometimes get the feeling you were almost, well almost trying to get your own back on the world, would that be true?

Yes, it would. Yes, it's true, that is.

And the older you've got, the more you've felt there was you had to get your own back for?

Yes. Why should I feel that, do you know?

Something happens when you're young, it gets exaggerated in your feelings perhaps, it's more important than you think it is, and——

No, it isn't more important than you think it is. It's the most important thing in the world, and you know it. . . .

Well, it may be or may not be, but you——

It is. I've never said this to no one before, not in all these years and years. No one's asked me, I suppose that's why. But now we're here at it, I might as well come out with it, it can't do any harm to anyone else, they're all dead. Have another bun.

No thank you.

You remember I told you, a long time ago, about the man in the cemetery I used to meet, and how my mother wouldn't let me go out with him? Well . . . it wasn't quite true, I mean in the way I told it to you. Oh, she saw us all right and she said I wasn't to have anything to do with him, that was true. But it was because he was my father, that was why. She said 'He's your father and he's been in trouble with the police for interfering with girls, don't you have no more to do with him.' So I went to my grandmother and I asked her if it was true, if it *was* my father and if he *had* been in trouble for that, and she said Yes it was and yes he had, and she said 'Don't you have anything to do with him.'

It was too late. It was much much too late. I'd been going in the woods with him for weeks every day on my way home from school. Every time I'd let him do it he'd given me a bag of sweets. I hadn't known who he was, but he knew me, that was how he knew my name and everything.

He was waiting for me again that same day after school, and on the way home when we got to the path where we always turned off in to the woods I burst out crying and I wouldn't go. I said 'You're my father, aren't you, you're my father?'

He pulled back his hand and he hit me right across the face, and he said 'Don't you tell anyone about what we've been doing, do you understand? Because if you do, you could go to prison for doing it—you could go to prison, do you understand?' And he ran off down the lane and I never saw him again. I've never let a man lay a finger on me, from that day to this.

Well, I'll put these buns back in the tin again, shall I, till tomorrow?

* * * * * *

She had carried it in private shame for nearly fifty years, seeking the punishment she felt she deserved, and rarely failing to find it. She is too old now to be helped much by sympathy or understanding; too old to bother much now whether she gets it. She wants to be left alone: and if a prison cell is the only place she can have solitude, she does not very much mind.

APPENDIX

*

MILLIE

*

> A certain smile, a certain face,
> Can lead an unsuspecting heart
> On a merry chase;
> A fleeting glance
> Can say so many lovely things;
> Suddenly you know why my heart sings . . .

It's a Johnny Mathis number, it's always been my very special favourite. I had my face up against the cool iron bars of the cell window and I was singing it out into the summer night to keep my spirits up. That was as much of the song as I knew then; and suddenly there came this man's voice, a marvellous rich voice tone it was, singing the rest of it back to me . . .

> You love a while, and when love goes
> You try to hide the tears inside
> With a cheerful pose;
> But in the hush of night
> Exactly like a bitter-sweet refrain
> Comes that certain smile to haunt your heart again.

'Oh gosh!' I shouted out, 'that's absolutely terrific, it is. Whoever you are, you've got a really wonderful voice. Where are you? How long are you in for?'

He said 'You can't see me, sweetheart, I'm over the other side of the wall in the men's block. And I'm doing four years. What about singing it together now, O.K.?'

So we sang it all through again together, and it really bucked me up it did. After that I got down from the window and lay on the bed and went to sleep. Up till then I'd been feeling so miserable and unhappy and lonely in that dreadful prison, I was quite sure I was going to lie awake all night long crying. If I hadn't sung that little song and then heard that man singing it back to me, I think I'd have broken my heart that night. I've often wondered since then who he was, and what he was in prison for. Perhaps he'd done something very bad. But that night he was just another human being in prison like me, and he certainly did me a good turn by singing back to me.

* * * * * *

Carol Dean, Diane Richards, Joe Bishop, Miss McDonald and Janie Preston: they had all been in prison because they had committed offences for which they had been caught, charged and convicted. What they did broke the Law and was criminal, and they were sent to prison as a punishment for it. But there are also people in prison who have committed no crimes and are not criminals. They are there only because society has not yet found anything better to do with them.

Millie Jackson was one. The incident she describes happened when she was put in prison two weeks after her sixteenth birthday.

She was born a few years after the end of the 1939-45 war, the illegitimate child of a Lincolnshire farm-girl and an American negro airman. She has never seen her father and does not even know his name: probably he has no idea of his daughter's existence. A year later

Millie's mother gave birth to another half-caste child by a different father; after another two or three years she had the opportunity of marrying a garage-mechanic and making what she described to Millie in later years as 'a fresh start'—that is, beginning a new and all-white family. She took it. Millie and her half-brother, left in the care of a distant relative who had neither the ability nor the desire to keep them, were soon moved to a County Council Children's Home (not in Lincolnshire), and not long afterwards transferred into the keeping of a charitable organisation which devotes itself to the upbringing of abandoned or orphaned children.

When Millie told me her story, she was living with her six-month-old baby in a small furnished room in Battersea. Not yet eighteen, with dark shining eyes and beautiful even white teeth, she talked about the deprived childhood she had experienced with great zest and amusement. Everything that had ever happened to her was always described as either 'interesting' or 'funny now I look back on it'. She never expressed anger at any of the indignities that had been done to her in the name of welfare, nor sorrow at the lonely years which must always have been her experience. Once I asked her if she ever felt bitter. 'Good Lord no, what about?' she said, laughing; and then, picking up her gurgling baby from where it was rolling happily on the floor she said: 'How could anyone be bitter, anyway, when life had brought them something as lovely as my Sylvie?'

* * * * * *

Really it's been very interesting my life, well I think it has, in the way it's turned out. I mean my mother had me when she didn't want a baby, and then I had Sylvie when I didn't really want a baby, or at least

I wasn't married: in a way it's almost been the same for both of us, hasn't it? I've really felt I've understood my mother a lot better now I've had Sylvie, knowing what she was feeling before she had her baby and all the rest of it. I think it helps you to understand people, having a baby, especially if you're young. My mother had me when she was very young, she must have been only about as old as I am too, so that's another thing makes it rather interesting, isn't it, the way the pattern's been the same?

Anyway, I'm going to try and keep it in order for you, so I'll start right back at the beginning, shall I? Well the very first thing I can remember is standing on a big green lawn with all the trees round, and the woman tugging at my hand and saying 'Come along dear, there's a good girl, this way now.' And I was trying to kick her ankle, I was a real little devil.

Another woman was pulling at Sammy, my half-brother, and taking him off in the opposite direction and saying 'Come along dear' too to him. We were both of us yelling our heads off because we didn't want to be separated from each other; a really shocking noise we were making, screeching and carrying on something dreadful! It must have looked really funny if anyone had been passing. They would have wondered what on earth these two women were doing to us, wouldn't they?

I didn't see Sammy for years and years after that, not until I was quite grown up, about twelve or thirteen. We neither of us knew each other at first, it was a scream; we were both put into this sitting-room at one of the children's homes and we didn't know why, we'd no idea we were related, we just sat and looked at each other for ages and didn't say a word! Then one of the housemothers came in and said 'Well

Sammy, and what do you think of your sister?' He said 'All right', and when the woman had gone out we both burst out laughing and couldn't stop.

Now then, I've gone right off the point again, haven't I, where was I? Oh yes, being taken away from him when we got put into the Home. I think that was because they had to have the boys in one place and the girls in another. It was a huge place, all divided up into separate houses, each in charge of housemothers and fathers, really like a whole town on its own it was. It's not surprising I didn't see Sammy again for so long, is it?

Everything was very strict in the house I was in, we all had to go to church a lot and be in at a certain time every night, depending on how old we were. There were about twelve of us altogether in the house, all girls; three others were partly-coloured like me. We didn't have a housefather, we had two housemothers; one was Irish and smoked a lot, and the other was a woman called Miss Hargreaves. She was very thin and mannish with close-cropped hair, and in the evenings she used to give us all Ju-Jitsu lessons, so that we'd be able to look after ourselves if a man ever attacked us, she said. I shouldn't think any man would ever have wanted to attack her, I can tell you that, a right old Les she was.

When I was about ten she told me one day to get myself washed and dressed-up nicely because my mother was coming to see me. I put on my pink party dress, and had my hair combed which I hated; and then I sat at the front-room window watching for her coming along the drive. I sat and sat and nobody appeared, and then Miss Hargreaves came and said 'I'm sorry Millie but your mother won't be visiting, after all, she's missed her train.' I was really fed-up about it, having my hair combed and everything; I can remember kicking my feet and putting on a real paddy about it, you know? A few days later Miss Hargreaves gave me a lovely big Easter egg which she said my mother had sent me. But I bet she hadn't, I bet she bought it for me herself.

Poor old thing, she's dead now, Miss Hargreaves. She was taken ill not long after that, and she died and we never saw her again. The Irish woman was very upset about it, in fact we all were, we all cried like mad about it, because she was so nice.

One day a couple came who wanted to have a girl to go and live with them, and I was chosen. I went to their house a few times for tea, and then I went to stay with them on a month's trial. Honestly, it was shocking —on Sundays I had to go to church with them in the morning, Sunday School on my own in the afternoon, and church again with them at night. We had prayers every evening before we went to bed, grace before every meal—it was like living in a monastery— or do I mean a convent? I got really awkward and nasty about it, you know, wouldn't eat anything at mealtimes, sulked and wouldn't speak to any of them. At the end of the month they said they were fed-up with me, which isn't surprising is it, and I had to go back to the Home.

At least that's where I thought I was going back to, but instead I was moved up north to another one, in Cumberland I think it was. God knows what the idea of that was, I don't, but it was a terrible place.

(The idea, I later discovered after some independent enquiry, was quite simple. But as it was based on ignorance of English geography, it was also completely useless. It had been felt by the manager of the Home that as the mother had failed to make the journey to the south to see Millie, she might

make an effort if Millie were moved nearer to her in 'th north'. But where Millie was sent to in Cumberland was in fact a good deal further away from her mother than the home in the south had been. T.P.)

I was really unhappy up there, I'd no friends or anything, and I wanted to get back to where I'd been before, but they wouldn't let me go. It was a big gloomy old house up on top of a hill. We weren't allowed to call the housemother 'Auntie' like we'd done at the other Home, we had to address her all the time as 'Matron'. There were about twenty children there, boys and girls, of all ages. We all went together every morning in a long crocodile to the school, about a mile away it was, down in the next village.

One day I left my cardigan at school, and the next morning at breakfast the matron ticked me off about it and said 'Don't you come back without it today Millie, or you'll really be in trouble.' When I got to school I couldn't find it anywhere. I was really frightened, I didn't dare go back to the Home after what matron had said. I hung around in the village until long after it was dark, looking in the shop windows until they turned the lights out, and then I went and sat on a bench by a horse-trough in the High Street. After a while a policeman came up on a bicycle, he said 'Aren't you from Hill House?' and he took me back there, and I got whacked with a slipper by one of the assistants for staying out.

In the summer two of the boys from the school we went to asked me and another girl if we'd like to go and see Blackpool illuminations with them one night, if they could borrow a van off someone they knew. This other girl was in the orphanage with me, and we both said Yes we'd like to go, but we'd have to be back before midnight otherwise we'd really get into terrible trouble. At the orphanage up to midnight it was trouble; after that it was terrible trouble, you know? The boys said it would be all right, they'd see we weren't late, and off we went.

Of course we might have known—the van broke down. Not on the way back but on the way there, so we never made it and it was about two o'clock when we did eventually get in. Oh, did we get it in the neck—and we hadn't even seen the illuminations either! But matron more or less made up for it, she went most of the different colours herself. Me and my friend could hardly keep our faces straight, you'd have thought we'd committed the Mail Train Robbery the way she was going on!

By now I was thirteen, and a big girl for my age, and getting really to be one of the ringleaders of any trouble that was going at the orphanage. So they decided they'd better move me to another one, right down on the south coast this one was.

I went to a real toffee-nosed school, all the girls wore terrible round felt hats and blazers and talked without opening their mouths properly, oh it was awful. What with me being half-coloured as well, I felt really out of everything, really on my own and with no one to talk to and no one at the new Home either. All the other children knew one another there and I knew no one.

The housemother was Scotch and she was very religious. She said if only I prayed hard enough I'd be saved; but I didn't know what it was I was supposed to get saved from. There was just one boy in the whole place who was nice to me: and that was the boy who came to the Home every day at tea-time delivering the bread. I used to wait for him at the gate so I could talk to him, he was really nice and friendly.

He asked me would I go to the pictures with him, and I said I would. I knew if I asked the housemother she wouldn't let me go out with a boy, so I just disappeared after tea and went down in the town and met him. We went to the pictures, we saw a really good film, it was called *Beat The Devil*; then we went a walk along the promenade. We were skylarking about in the shelters, and doing a bit of kissing and cuddling. Then he said to me 'Will you spend the night with me?' so I said 'Yes all right, if you can find somewhere for us to go where we can sleep.'

He said there was a hut up on top of the cliffs, something to do with a quarry up there I think it was. Off we went, climbing up these cliffs in the moonlight, hand-in-hand, oh it was terribly romantic! When we got inside the hut, there was just a dirty stone floor and a bench, so we made ourselves as comfortable as we could on our coats. Laugh! Oh dear it was so funny, it was just plain ridiculous! We were both so cold, you see, we sat and shivered with our arms round each other all night. We could hear mice running about, and owls hooting outside, it was really frightening. We both felt absolutely cross-eyed in the morning with the cold and not being able to sleep. Talk about young love, it wasn't in it, honestly, it was a scream!

I went straight to school and got there at the proper time—but of course half way through morning, I was sent for to go to the headmaster's study. There was the Scotch housemother with him, both doing their nuts, and I had to be taken straight back to the Home. When I got there, two plain-clothes police, a man and a woman, were waiting for me.

Of course then I'd no idea what it was all about, you see; I only cottoned-on about a year or so ago that this boy was 18 and I was 13, and they were after him for doing it with a girl under age. Anyway, as I say, there these two were in the housemother's office waiting for me. They both started asking me questions together, then the man suddenly said 'Did you have sexual intercourse, yes or no?'

I knew what 'sex' meant but I'd no idea about the other word, I'd never heard it before. So I said 'Yes I think so.' The plain-clothes policewoman looked at me, then she looked at the man as though he was some kind of idiot, and she said to him 'Why don't you go off and talk to the housemother?'

The moment he'd got out of the door she whipped round on me and she said 'Did he have his thing out?' Honestly, I wasn't pulling her leg, I really misunderstood her: I looked past her at the door that was closing and I said 'I don't know, I couldn't see.' She said 'Not him, you silly girl! The boy who was in the shed with you last night!'

Well it's too rude to tell you the rest of what she said; but of course, nothing had happened that shouldn't have, I was still a virgin, though this woman wouldn't believe me. I had to go and be examined by a doctor; he told me to get up on the couch and he said 'It won't hurt' but it damn well did.

I'd no idea why they were making all this fuss about a bit of fun that hadn't done anyone any harm, and I got mixed-up about the whole thing, you know, ashamed, afraid, thinking I'd done something terrible and all the rest of it. It took me years to get over it and find out that really sex is very nice.

So after all that, even though nothing had been wrong they decided I was in need of care and protection, and I was sent to a Remand Home for two weeks. Nobody came to see me and tell me anything, I was just dumped in there and left to get on with trying to find out from other girls in it exactly what was going on. Some of them were well-up in everything, of course. One of them said 'Well if they're going to send you to an Approved School, you ought to see it's for something worth being sent away for, not just for a cold night sitting on a stone floor in a shed.'

All I knew about Approved Schools was they were supposed to be for bad girls, and I honestly couldn't see what I'd done that was so terrible. All the other girls in the Remand Home seemed to be there for stealing and things like that. Anyway after a fortnight I was taken to court and the magistrate said 'The Remand Home have given a good report on you, so you'll be sent to an Approved School for four years.'

Four years in an Approved School! You've got to laugh; I thought my God, what would they have given me if the Remand Home report had been bad—twenty years in Australia? I felt really annoyed with everybody again, I said to myself Well I'm not stopping in in any Approved School. I'd been looking forward to the time when I could leave school when I was fourteen, and start earning my own living and not have to live in an orphanage any more. There was only another year to go, and then I'd be free—or at least that's what I thought, and then they came up with those four years at Approved School for me. I was livid, I was; it looked as though other people were going to go on directing my life for me for ever.

I was taken from court to a classifying centre, where they kept me for three or four weeks and gave me all sorts of tests and things—intelligence tests to see if I'd got any brains, and more physical tests just to make sure again that I wasn't pregnant. I was tested so many times for that I got the feeling sometimes I was unusual because I wasn't. Being pregnant seemed the normal thing, and anyone else was a freak. After a t me you begin to think it's almost expected of you, you're not playing the game if you don't give them the result they're waiting for, you know?

I was put into one of the Approved Schools in the Home Counties. Oh it was shocking, it really was, if you'd seen me you'd have died laughing, I looked such a sight! I had a horrible pale blue dress with short sleeves, all washed out because so many people had worn it before, big black lace-up shoes and little white socks—you've never seen anything like it. Then for best we had coloured dresses and blazers, but we were only supposed to put those on on Sundays.

The other girls there were all very nice but compared with them I was so green it wasn't true. Some of the things they'd done to get put in there, it was fantastic! Mind you I think a lot of it was exaggerated, but all the same they were really rough tough girls, some of them. Great fun to be with, of course, though, they really were. They used to fight like hell—I'm sorry, I mean they used to fight a lot—it was better than the wrestling on television sometimes.

One of the best fighters was a girl called Tessa, she wasn't frightened of anybody, and one day she said to me 'I'm having it away to London tonight, Millie, are you coming? My boyfriend's picking me up in the village in his car.' I said 'Ooh yes, lovely, I'll be ready'—and away we went after supper, up over the fence and down the road. No boy friend in a car though; if there ever was one, he didn't show up. Tessa said we'd better start walking. Oh my feet! In those great big heavy shoes, they were killing me: I think we'd only got about four miles when a police car came up behind us. Was I glad to see them, I said to them 'Now we can ride back in comfort, I d never have made it if I'd had to walk.'

For that I got sent straight back again to the classifying centre. The woman who ran it said 'I'm really disappointed in you Millie, I thought you were going to make a go of it.' I said 'I did try to make a go of it but I couldn't get far enough.' Not very witty and not much help either, because she just sniffed and said 'We'll have to send you somewhere else that you can't get out of so easily.'

So off I go again, this time to another Approved School, up in the Midlands. When I got there I was taken for an interview with the Headmistress; quite a mild-looking little woman she was, with those funny glasses—what are they called, 'pince-nez' or something? —and grey hair scraped back in a bun. She was sitting behind a desk and when I went in she smiled at me and said 'Sit down, Millie dear—now I want to tell you that if you create any trouble while you are here, I personally will kill you with my bare hands.'

I thought 'Ooh, charming, what an introduction!' Laugh—it was the funniest opening I'd ever heard, but she really meant it, she did. After a few days I'd chummed-up with another girl called Sheila, who said she wanted to get to Sheffield where her boyfriend was living, and get him to help her. So I said 'I'll come with you, then' and we made arrangements to leave at the week-end after dinner on Sunday, when most of the staff were asleep and we were supposed to be having a walk round the grounds on our own. We climbed up a tree and got over the wall, hung about until it was dark, then hitched a lift in a lorry off a very nice chap who said he didn't envy anyone in Approved School, he'd nearly been sent to one when he was a kid himself.

When we got to the flat where Sheila's boy friend was

living, it was just like a scene in a play, very dramatic it was. There was a party going on, about six or seven boys and girls lolling about in this flat, drinking and listening to records. We rang the bell and when he opened the door he didn't want to let us in; we thought it was because we looked like a couple of kids in our school-macs and uniforms. Anyway we pushed in past him; and then Sheila stopped right in the middle of the room and pointed at a blonde on the couch with her legs up. She said 'You've got my best dress on, you bitch—take it off.' This girl was living with the boy of course, and using all Sheila's things. Sheila said 'Come on, take it off now—or I'll have it off you.' And this blonde stood up, she put her hand up behind her back and pulled the zipper, and the dress just fell down round her ankles and she stepped out of it. Sheila took a flying kick at it on the floor and sent it into the fireplace; then she turned round and took a kick at the girl who yelled and sat down holding her leg; then she turned round again and took a kick at the boy. He just stood still and winced. Then she said to me, 'Come on, Millie' and out we went.

I said to her 'Ooh, that was terrific, you ought to be on the stage, you should, it was really dramatic.' Of course we had to walk round the streets of Sheffield the rest of the night, and naturally the police saw us and picked us up.

I was expecting to be personally killed by the Headmistress when I got back, but she'd caught 'flu and the Deputy was in charge. 'Millie, Millie!' she said 'Whatever were you thinking of, taking a nice quiet girl like Sheila off with you just when she was so happy here?' I thought 'Well blimey—who's kidding who?'—did you ever hear anything like it!

I hung around waiting for the Headmistress to

recover and get on with killing me, but before she got back in action I was suddenly told one day to get my coat, I was going to be taken on the train to Birmingham by one of the assistants. When we got there I was put on another train by her, given a ticket, and told my mother would be meeting me at the other end. Nobody'd told me a thing about it beforehand; they just stuck me on the train and I didn't know whether I was supposed to stay with my mother for a day, a week, for ever, or what.

In fact I didn't even really want to go and meet her at all; but then I thought I might as well go and see what she looked like, anyway. Though as far as I was concerned anyone could have come up to me at the other end and said 'I'm your mother' and I wouldn't have known the difference.

That's just what this woman did say when I got off the train. I suppose she recognised me because I was half-coloured. She was all right, just an ordinary little woman, I felt a bit sorry for her really, she was so embarrassed. She took me to the house she was living in, and introduced me to her husband and their three children, and said she'd been given permission to keep me for a week's holiday.

Really I don't know who was more bored after the first few days, her or me, because we'd nothing to talk about and nothing in common. I was quite relieved when the end of the week came and I could go back to the Approved School, and I'm sure she was too.

When I did get back, I was only there about two hours and then I was told I was being transferred to another one up in Northumberland, and I was taken straight to it the same day. I was feeling so cheesed-off, fed-up and browned-off when I arrived that I didn't make the faintest attempt to co-operate with anybody,

I just sulked. And the first chance I got I escaped yet again, only this time on my own, through a bedroom window one morning after breakfast.

I went into a transport café down in the town, and there was a negro lorry driver there, so I asked him if he'd give me a lift. 'Where to?' he said. 'I don't mind,' I said, 'Just anywhere that you're going.'

'Oh no' he said, 'I can't do a thing like that to a young girl like you, just drop you off anywhere and not care about what happens to you. But I've got a sister' he said, 'over in Liverpool which is where I'm going now—I'll take you to her if you like.'

So I went with him, and she was really nice his sister was, she had a husband and two lovely little children, and they let me stay with them for about three weeks. I got a job in a café down by the docks, and I got quite keen on this lorry driver. He was a really nice fellow, his name was Toby, and he wasn't all that much older than me, he was only about 20. He was my first real proper boy friend, and after a while we moved out of his sister's into a couple of rooms of our own. It was really lovely, it was, a very happy time.

One day two detectives came in the café, I didn't see them come in because I had my back to them behind the counter. One of them said 'Hello Millie'— and of course without thinking I turned round and said, 'Oh hello'. That was it, I'd put my foot right in it, hadn't I? They took me off to the police station, and they kept me there for hours. If there'd been any crime done in Liverpool in the past ten years that they didn't ask me if I knew anything about, it can only have been because they couldn't remember it. I think after a time they must have thought I was crazy or something, because I just couldn't stop laughing at all the ridiculous things they kept asking me—what about the Aintree Post Office job, what about the ring of Arabic dope-peddlers? All things like that, dead serious they were about it too; who they thought I was I don't know.

Then I was taken off to a Remand Home again. I thought the previous one I'd been in was tough, but this one made it seem like a convent. They really had got half the Arabic dope-peddling ring in there, and most of the Aintree Post Office robbers' girls too, I should think. I arrived just as a mass-break-out was being planned, so of course I put my name down for it. A few days later the whole place more or less exploded.

We all barricaded ourselves in the dining-room, smashed up all the tables and chairs and piled them against the windows, oh it was shocking. They sent for the police to come and get us out, and a policeman climbed up and pushed a window open and got his head through. One of the girls was standing on a pile of tables near the window with a big metal tray, and she started wanging it down on his head. It sounded like Big Ben striking, it was an absolute scream. I don't think it can have hurt him because he had his helmet on, but the noise was tremendous, it must have half-deafened him. You should have seen his face!

Then some idiot set fire to a pile of paper and cardboard cartons, and the police really had to break the door down before the whole place went up in smoke. They took us all off to court in a van and asked for a remand in custody—and we were all taken to Strangeways prison. So that was how I got there.

The woman taking particulars in the reception part said to me what's your name and all the rest of it, and then she asked me my age, so I told her what it was—

sixteen. 'Sixteen!' she said, 'How shocking! You're only sixteen and already you're in a place like this!' I laughed, I said 'Well blimey, I didn't ask to be brought here, did I?' She said 'It's nothing to laugh about—and you must have asked *for* it, mustn't you, or else you wouldn't be here.'

Then they took me up to a cell and locked me in. It was just like you see in pictures, a little room with bare walls and a bed, a wooden chair and a table, a jug of cold water and a basin and a chamber pot, and a barred window high up in the wall.

It was terribly hot, it was summer, I'd nothing to read and no one to talk to. They switched the light off about nine o'clock, and I felt really miserable and unhappy and lonely, which isn't like me really. So I climbed up on the chair and put my face against the bars, they were lovely and cool, and then I started to sing that song.

And that nice man started to sing it back to me.

* * * * * * *

When I came up in court a few days later, I got sent to Borstal Training. They don't give you any length of time, they simply say 'From between two to four years'. And where did I go after that? You'll laugh when I tell you: I went straight back to the prison again, and I was kept there for another two months. You're only allowed to mix with the other prisoners on exercise at first, but then after a few weeks you can go to dances together, film shows, social evenings and so on. I made friends with a coloured girl there who was in for murder; I thought she was very nice. Some of the prostitutes and thieves were nice too, especially the younger ones; but I didn't get on so well with the really old ones, they were so grumpy and didn't like you being noisy.

Then after I'd been there three months in the prison I was told that at last I was going to Borstal. I thought 'Ooh good, I hope it's somewhere really nice, right out in the country or something.' My idea of Borstal was always a big house in the country miles from anywhere, isn't it yours?

You'll never guess where I went—into another prison! They'd decided that in view of my history of running away I'd have to go to what they call a 'closed' Borstal, by which they mean simply part of an ordinary prison, that's all: you live in a cell just like anyone else.

But I was very very lucky, because not long after I got there I was taken ill and had to go into the hospital, and that's where I spent most of my sentence. One of the nursing sisters there was really lovely, and ever so good to me. She lent me her radio set, brought me books, sent in soap and cigarettes and jigsaws from outside at Christmas, sat and talked to me—she was absolutely wonderful to me, she really was.

Well, being in a closed Borstal and being ill as well, there was no more running away for me. I had to stay where I was. After a year I was moved for a few months to another Borstal, a semi-secure one I think they called it, and then I was released. On licence, of course, but I don't mind that: my After-Care supervisor is very nice, she's a really lovely woman. I'm very fond of her, I go and talk to her whenever I like. She's just like my mum really, that's just how I think of her. It's daft isn't, it? But I do.

* * * * * * *

Do you ever feel bitter, Millie?
Good Lord no, what about? How could anyone be

bitter, anyway, when life has brought them something as lovely as my Sylvie? Pooh, she smells, she wants changing, don't you darling? Come on then, we'll soon have you right, won't we beautiful?

No, not really bitter, I don't think, ever. I used to, sometimes, just a bit when I was a kid in the orphanage. Especially when some of the older girls used to stay out at night and get into trouble the next morning, and the housemother used to say to them 'You've been with those horrible dirty coloured men again, haven't you?' I could hear her saying it to them, and it used to go right through me, you know?

Of course it's always been a bit difficult for me because I'm neither one thing nor the other, you see. I'm not white and I'm not a negro, and I don't fit in with either properly. I can never say 'These are the people I belong with.' My boy friend now, he's a Jamaican, he's Sylvie's dad and she's darker than I am, so perhaps she'll fit in better somewhere than me. But so long as she's happy, that's the main thing: and I'm certainly never going to put her in a home like I had to be. The only way that could happen would be if I was recalled to Borstal or something—and that'll never happen, so there's nothing to worry about.

I only got in there for running away from places. Now I'm old enough at last to live my own life outside and do what I like, so they can't touch me—only if I commit some crime or other, which I shan't ever do.

Did Borstal do you good or harm?

It's difficult to say. It could have done me a lot of harm, I think, if I'd let it. All the girls in there when they left they used to shout out to one another 'Cheerio, see you in Holloway.' They'd no intention of going straight, most of them; but then of course they were in for things like stealing or prostituting or house-breaking. You pick up a terrific lot of knowledge about how to lead a life of crime in there, hints on how to knock-off jewellery and furs and all the rest: that's all they ever talk about.

I found it interesting to listen to, but somehow it just never attracted me one bit, I never thought 'Yes, I'll try that when I go out.' I knew exactly what I wanted to do, I wanted to get a job and settle down and find a nice boy friend to live with, and have a baby.

And you know, when they put my Sylvie in my arms in the hospital, that was the happiest moment of my life. She's all different shades of brown, but I think she's beautiful—beautiful, bee-yoo-tiful, aren't you love, yes you are, really bee-yoo-yoo-tiful, you are!

Life's terrifically interesting, isn't it?

BIBLIOGRAPHY

The following books, pamphlets and articles were consulted:-

ADAM, H. L.: *Women & Crime* (Werner Laurie, 1912)
AHNSJO, SVEN: *Delinquency in Girls* (Stockholm, 1932);
Association of Heads of Approved Schools: Girls in Approved Schools (1954)
BARTON, RUSSELL: *Institutional Neuroses* (Wright, 1959)
BISHOP, CECIL: *Women & Crime* (London, 1931)
BRIT. MEDICAL ASSOCIATION: *The Unstable Adolescent Girl* (B.M.J., 1946)
BROWN, CAROLINE: *Lost Girls* (Gollancz, 1955)
BRYAN, HELEN: *Inside*
BURT, CYRIL: *The Young Delinquent*
BUXTON, J. & TURNER, M.: *Gate Fever* (Cresset Press, 1962)
CENTRAL AFTER-CARE ASSOCIATION: *Annual Reports, 1949-62*
CHESTERTON, G.: *Women of The Underworld* (S. Paul, 1928)
FEDDERN, P.: *Searchlights on Delinquency* (Imago, 1949)
FERNALD, HAYES & DAWLEY: *A Study of Delinquents* (N.Y., 1920)
FIELD, XENIA: *Under Lock and Key* (M. Parrish, 1964)
GIBBENS, T. C. N. & PRINCE, J.: *Shoplifting* (I.S.T.D., 1963)
GILES, F. T.: *The Criminal Law* (Penguin Books, 1954)
GLUECK, S. & E.: *500 Delinquent Women* (Knopf, 1934)
HARDING, M. E.: *The Way of All Women* (Longmans, 1935)
HAYS, PETER: *New Horizons in Psychiatry* (Penguin Books, 1964)
HENDERSON, A. & GILLESPIE: *Textbook of Psychiatry* (O.U.P.)
HENRY, JOAN: *Who Lie in Gaol* (Gollancz, 1952)
HIBBERT, CHRISTOPHER: *The Roots of Evil* (Weidenfeld, 1963)
HOME OFFICE: *Prisons & Borstals* (1960);
Criminal Statistics (Annually)
HOWARD, D. L.: *The English Prisons* (Methuen, 1960)
JENKINS, ELIZABETH: *Six Criminal Women* (S. Low, 1949)
LABOUR PARTY: *Crime, A Challenge To Us All* (1964)
LOMBROSO, CESARE: *The Female Offender* (London, 1895)

LONDON FEMALE PENITENTIARY: *16th Annual Report* (1823)
LUCAS, NETLEY: *Crook Janes* (S. Paul, 1926)
McCALL, CICELY: *They Always Come Back* (1938)
MAGISTRATES ASSOCIATION: *Training in Girls' Borstals* (1951)
MANNHEIM, H.: *Social Aspects of Crime* (Allen & Unwin, 1940)
MARTIN, J. B.: *Break Down The Walls* (Gollancz, 1955)
MILLER, DEREK: *Growth To Freedom* (Tavistock, 1964)
POLLACK, OTTO: *The Criminality of Women* (U.S.A., 1950)
ROBINSON, F. W.: *Female Life in Prison* (1894)
RUCK, S. K. (ed.): *Paterson On Prisons* (Muller, 1951)
SCOTTISH HOME & HEALTH DEPT.: *Prisons in Scotland* (1963)
SIZE, MARY: *Prisons I Have Known* (Allen & Unwin, 1957)
SMITH, ANN D.: *Women in Prison* (Stephens, 1962)
STAFFORD-CLARK, D.: *Psychiatry For Students* (Allen & Unwin, 1964)
SULLIVAN, K.: *Girls Who Go Wrong* (Gollancz, 1956)
WALKER, NIGEL: *Crime and Punishment in Britain* (Edin. U.P., 1965)
WOODSIDE, M.: *Women Drinkers in Holloway* (Brit. J. Crim., 1961)
WOODWARD, MARY: *Low Intelligence and Delinquency* (I.S.T.D., 1955)